MY LIFE MY POWER
IT'S TIME WE ALL STAND UP

This publication is designed to provide accurate and authoritative information in regard to the subject matter covered. It is sold with the understanding that the publisher is not engaged in rendering professional services. If professional advice or other expert assistance is required, the services of a competent professional person should be sought.

Written by: Daniel Puder, David Puder MD, Brittney Lozano, Jackson Wong, Tina Morse, James Ream, Carolyn Quijano RD MS

Cover Design and Ninja Layout: Mac Cook

Editor: Michelle Dotter and Bobby Shariat

Cover Photographer: Jason Foy

Cover Models: Daniel Puder, Kenton Duty, Carmen Ruiz, Jessica Berry, Joanna Kan, Antoine Domino, Anthony Mercado

PUBLISHER'S DISCLAIMER

The material in this book is for informational purposes only. As each individual's situation is unique, you should consult a health care provider before undertaking the diet, exercise, and lifestyle techniques described in this book. The authors and publishers expressly disclaim responsibility for any adverse effects that may result from the use or application of the information contained in this book.

My Life My Power Biography

My Life My Power is a nonprofit organization which was founded in 2010 by Daniel Puder to combat many crises harming today's youth. After hearing the tragic stories of children and teenagers who committed suicide due to bullying and intimidation, Daniel felt a personal connection to the situation knew that something needed to be done to change the mindset of our youth. Rather than simply saying a few public words about this issue, Daniel was compelled to create a program geared toward our youth, that could be implemented in the school system in order to prevent more tragedies.

While My Life My Power began as an anti-bullying program, it has since expanded to also address a wide range of other problems that children and teenagers confront daily basis, all of which require increased awareness. We know that at the heart of each child has the desire to succeed in life. The My Life My Power program has been specifically designed to teach our youth the importance of goal-setting, mentoring, character building, and leadership in order to develop a positive mindset toward themselves, their peers, authority figures, and that may ultimately lead to their own success and increased happiness in life.

The My Life My Power book consists of two parts. The first part called "My Life" takes the reader on a personal journey of self-discovery to help them figure out what they want to achieve in life. The second part, called "My Power" provides the tools necessary to implement the realizations from the first part. Readers who have any further questions regarding the topics discussed in this book are encouraged to speak with their parents, mentors, and faith leaders. For more information, please visit our website at www.MyLifeMyPower.org.

DANIEL PUDER

Undefeated MMA Heavyweight Fighter

WWE's $1,000,000 Tough Enough Champion

Founder of My Life My Power

Daniel Puder made a name for himself as a professional undefeated heavyweight mixed martial arts fighter and won WWE's $1,000,000 Tough Enough Championship on Smackdown on UPN. After the WWE, Puder went back to mixed martial arts and was featured on KRON, Fox Sports, NBC, *Men's Fitness*, and *Sports Illustrated*.

Puder has balanced his athletic career and business ventures with another passion: giving back to the community. He started his first charity when he was nineteen years old: Puder Strength Training, which helped train kids during the summer. In 2009, he became a Shriner so that he could spend more time mentoring kids within the Shriner's hospitals around the world.

Puder has also traveled around the United States donating his time by speaking to children and teenagers for the National Police Athletic League (PAL).

Puder founded My Life My Power in 2010 to help spread a message of self-worth, accountability, and respect for today's youth. Puder is committed to installing the My Life My Power program into every school in the United States in order to ensure a more successful future for our youth.

In 2011, Puder branched out into the business world and he began working as the Director of Youth Programs for a startup company based out of southern California called, CUshop.org.

To help support My Life My Power, please visit www.MyLifeMyPower.org and join the cause today!

DAVID PUDER, M.D.

Dr. David Puder attended the University of California, Berkeley, and graduated with a degree in Molecular and Cell Biology. During his time at UC Berkeley, he was a member of the rowing team for four years and during his senior year, his team won the national championship, David's boat won the PAC-10, as well as being the second fastest boat in the nation.

David also developed his leadership skills by becoming a leader in Athletes in Action and working on various research projects and marketing videos. After college, David attended Loma Linda Medical School where he scored in the top 5% of all medical students in the nation on standardized tests. During his time here, David was the primary author on a research project that looked into new ways of performing kidney surgery.

David also helped lead the effort to adopt a hospital in Haiti, and personally traveled to Haiti four times during this endeavor. After the earthquake in Haiti, David worked as doctor in a Haitian emergency room in which he organized the pharmacy and coordinated efforts to get supplies into the island. While there, he made several small documentaries of his experiences. While in medical school, David volunteered as a chaplain at the San Bernardino Juvenile Hall to share his faith and encourage kids to set goals and overcome adversity.

In 2010, David became a medical doctor and completed his medical internship at Kettering Medical Center in Ohio. Currently, he is finishing his residency at Loma Linda Hospital in psychiatry, helping patients who struggle with issues such as suicide, depression, and addiction.

BRITTNEY LOZANO

Brittney Lozano is the Executive Director of My Life My Power. In 2009, Brittney received a Bachelor of Science degree in Apparel Design and Merchandising with a minor in business marketing from California State University, Northridge. Brittney grew up in a family of educators. Her father has been a chief administrator for over 25 years and her mother and sister are both teachers.

Brittney has over five years experience in working with numerous children's programs and it was while working with youth that she discovered her true passion for helping young people reach their full potential. Using the guidance and values taught to her by her parents, which are similar to the tools provided in this book, Brittney has been a role model and mentor to young people of all ages.

With Brittney's strong leadership skills and enthusiastic personality, the My Life My Power team has been able to create an effective program for our youth, as well as develop a marketing brand that will reach out to educators and parents alike, encouraging them to play an active role in creating a positive environment for future generations.

JACKSON WONG

Jackson Wong earned a Bachelor of Science degree from the University of California, San Diego. Since then, Jackson has had over five years of management experience in the retail industry, contributed his time and skills to film and entertainment projects, and gained inspiration through charity work. Most recently, Jackson has begun working with credit unions and he is a contributing author and mentor program director for My Life My Power. He is an expert in personal finance and has grown up in the generation where social media is widely used as a marketing tool and personal branding method. With his background in giving back to the community, his passion for helping kids, and his zest for mentoring others, Jackson utilizes his personal life experiences to help kids and young adults learn the importance of financial literacy and the value of personal branding through the My Life My Power Mentor Program.

TINA MORES

Tina Morse, MA, MFT, combines mind-body-spirit psychotherapy, life and relationship coaching, image consulting, yoga and movement therapy for personal healing and greater body awareness. She also provides natural gourmet recipes and ideas for nutritional healing and a healthy kitchen.

Tina has over 20 years of experience in the wellness industry, a Masters degree in counseling, psychology, and spiritual psychology, and is a licensed marriage and family therapist. She has worked as a treatment team member at Cedars-Sinai Hospital in both the Outpatient Psychiatry department and the Early Childhood Center, as well as a culinary wellness team member and advisor to the New Henry Ford Hospital.

Tina's media appearances include Maybelline, Max Factor and a film with John Cusack. She is an artist and creatively uses traditional and unique Eastern and Western treatment modalities that have helped her transform her own life. Her education and personal experiences inspire and empower others.

JAMES REAM

James Ream is a nineteen year veteran police officer of the Los Angeles School Police Department with a Bachelor's degree in Criminal Justice Management. James is ranked as Senior Police Officer, assigned as a field training officer, and is a founding member of the Los Angeles School Police Department's Special Response Team. James serves as the President of the Los Angeles School Police Association, where he has held this position for over a decade.

He is proudly serving, and has served, on several other boards including PORAC, COPFIRE, and LACOPS, as well as public charities such as the Los Angeles School Police Foundation, the Golden Badge Foundation, the Friends of Safe Schools Los Angeles charity and he also donates his time to My Life My Power as the Director of Operations. James has also served as the National Conference Director for the National Association of School Safety and Law Enforcement Officers (NASSLEO) and is currently the California representative for the National Association of School Resource Officers (NASRO), where he is able to share his experiences in the area of school safety.

Acknowledgments

My Life My Power would like to thank all of the celebrities, athletes, deputies, police officers, firefighters, teachers, counselors, corporations, and individuals who have taken a stand for our youth and their future. With your help, we can all change the world into a better place!

I would like to dedicate this book to everyone who has believed in me: my parents, Brent and Wanda Puder; brother David Puder; adopted family Harlan, Madeline and Taylor Gittin; Danny and Rachel Hoisman; my best friends Jason Foy, Amin Nikfar, Boe Trumbull, Dave Meltzer, Todd Burns, Corey Trevor, Bobby Shariat, Fr. Willy Raymond, and George Walker. Bobby Lopez with the SJPD and FOP, James Ream with LASPA and LASPD, Chief Steve Zipperman with LASPD and Rudy Perez, thank you for all of the direction and support. Also, my 1st and best coach, Javier Mendez from the American Kickboxing Academy.

A special thank you to Yori Uehara and Harvey Levin for providing me with worldwide media exposure through TMZ.

I would like to thank the following people for their support and generous donations toward My Life My Power: Michael King, Ron Tudor, John Paul DeJoria, Al Malnik, Vicki Walters, Linda and Harvey Vechery, the Richard Singh Family Foundation, the Nussdorf Family, and Vlado Footwear.

Most of all, I want to dedicate this book to my grandmother, **Dorothy "Grandma Knockout" Puder.** You have been a blessing in my life and I love you. Thank you for being the best grandmother in the world! Keep up the hard workouts!

TABLE OF CONTENTS

PART 1: MY LIFE

This is your life: This section will guide you toward figuring out what you want to make of yourself. I promise that if you learn to set goals, find good mentors, develop leadership skills, and have genuine character, you will be able to open doors to success in your life.

PART 2: MY POWER

This is your power: This section will show you how to develop healthy living habits and how to achieve and maintain self confidence to be empowered in your own life.

BY:

DANIEL PUDER

FOR OUR YOUTH!

Before you begin this book, be sure to take Quiz #1 located in the back of the book in Appendix A

After you complete this book, be sure to take Quiz #2 located in the back of the book in Appendix B

PART ONE: MY LIFE

"It doesn't matter what you're born with, it's what you do with what you have."

– Daniel Puder

CHAPTER 1
DISCOVER YOUR PASSIONS

by Daniel Puder

This program will take you on a journey of self-exploration. It's designed to help you create a road map for success and unlock your true potential. The beauty of discovering your passions is that you'll get out of it as much as you put into it—and with effort, you'll start seeing improvements in your quality of life in a short amount of time. In each lesson, I'll share stories from my personal life. I'll talk about how I've risen from hardship to the top by using these steps. While our hardships may differ, I have had to overcome some major hurdles in my life to become successful, and the major things I've learned is that happiness comes from within and with a combination of hard work, discipline, and vision, anything is possible.

As I write this, I'm hanging out at my buddy's house, thinking to myself: What do I like and dislike in my life? I'm going to start with waking up in the morning and starting the day. When I wake up in the morning, I usually lie in bed thinking that I'm going to make the most of this day.

There are a few things that finally get me out of bed:

1) I know I have a wonderful family that I love and who loves me back. Besides having a loving and supportive family in San Jose, I've also been "adopted" by a family here in Los Angeles that has taken me in as part of their family. They are healthy role models for how I want to live my life.

2) I'm happy I have a few great friends that I can rely on to be there for me when I'm in need.

3) I love my work and am excited for the challenges it brings every day. I've spent the past six years fighting and wrestling professionally. Currently, my day involves launching a startup company and building my charity. I've found my passions in life and have transformed them into a successful career. I surround myself only with ambitious people who are successful in life and strive to make the world a better place.

Next, I get up and take a shower to make sure I'm fresh and clean, followed by a healthy breakfast. After breakfast I check roughly 20 to 30 emails and text messages and plan my day. When I'm done, I get dressed. I used to only wear shorts and a t-shirt all day, even to most business meetings. I'm an undefeated MMA fighter so I could get away with wearing shorts to just about anything. However, now that I'm in the business world, I need to wear a suit most of the time. It's a change, but I'm starting to like looking like a business executive. I know to be the best I can be at my job I have to love it—so I'm learning to love wearing a suit because it's important to always look your best.

When I get to work, I work hard. I always have a pen and note pad with me so I can take notes on conversations and create to-do lists of things I need to accomplish. I have two rules for myself when I talk to people. Always be genuine and honest, and if I don't understand something, I just admit it and ask for clarification.

When I get off work, I usually hit the gym. I don't like to waste time so my workouts are fast and hard. After working out, I typically either go to a dinner meeting or have dinner with family or friends. If I'm going to a business dinner, I always set a goal for the meeting. If I'm out with family or friends, I make sure to enjoy my time; picking their brains for advice on life is always fun for me. When I get home, I jump on the computer and finish up everything that didn't get done during the day. As soon as everything is done I finally have time to relax and watch a movie.

Over the years, I've learned to surround myself with people who treat me well and to only work jobs that are fulfilling and make me excited to work each day. At this point in my life, I only focus on positive things. But that was not the case when I was growing up.

I was in Special Education classes as a kid because I had a learning disability. I wasn't keeping up with the rest of my first grade class so I was held back. I could read well, but my comprehension of the information was slow and I had a difficult time with spelling. I was teased daily, not to mention the fact that I was pushed around on the playground to the point where my brother and I had to team up to support each other. These days, people look at me and say, "Wow, Daniel, you're a huge, muscular, 235-pound professional fighter. How could you possibly have been pushed around?" Well, I haven't always been this way. I was one of the slowest kids in the sixth grade mile run. So not only was I in Special Education, I was one of the least athletic kids in school. On top of that, I ate too much junk food, which caused me to become overweight.

After barely passing sixth grade, I went to a private junior high school in Sunnyvale, California. I learned a lot in this school and started wrestling. With a lot of hard work, I excelled quickly in sports. During the first semester of my eighth grade, the school said they were going to fail me. I either had to leave or repeat the eighth grade. Let's just say this was not a fun decision and I was unhappy with my life. After thinking about it, I chose to go to public school, which ended up being a good decision. I made some new friends and learned that I love construction work. I started working a couple days a week with Habitat for Humanity, building houses for families in need. I was settling into my new school and was happy. Imagine my surprise when the principal called my parents in for a meeting and told them my math teacher was going to fail me. This school also wanted me to stay back a year! Fortunately, we were able to come up with a different solution—retake the same math class in high school. We all agreed and I barely made it into high school.

High school was a fresh beginning for me. I started making progress both socially and athletically with the guidance of a mentor. I was on the football team and the wrestling team, and I had friends in all different groups. Sports gave me opportunities and kept me motivated in school and life.

However, my outlook on life drastically changed in one day. When I was sixteen years old, I was yelled at by my athletic coach who was told false information about me by another student at my school. Unfortunately, I did not handle the situation in the right way and found myself involved in a physical altercation with this student which led to my being arrested. I was devastated—and honestly scared out of my mind. Imagine being stuck in a four-by-eight-foot cell with some kid who was hiding a weapon. I was so worried that I would get jumped by ten guys at once or that I would be locked up for a long time. This place was not a place I wanted to be. They told me when to wake up, when to shower, what to eat, and when to sleep. I knew without a doubt that this was not how I wanted to spend the rest of my life.

In looking back at that situation, I should have gone to the principal with a written complaint and had my parents follow up with the school. That way, my parents wouldn't have had to spend thousands of dollars on a lawyer, I would not have been locked up, and we all could have avoided the wasted time it took for that situation to be resolved. I made the decision to not fight on the street from that point forward.

When I got out of juvenile hall, my parents shocked me. I figured I would be grounded, but instead they said, "We think you've learned your lesson." I replied, "Absolutely!" and then I went back to school.

I had the good fortune of meeting UFC legend Frank Shamrock, who took me under his wing and taught me how to take my fighting out of the streets and into the ring. He told me he would train me at the American Kickboxing Academy for free as long as I promised not to get into any more fights. I made a complete transformation as both an athlete and a student and started working as hard in school as I did in sports. I excelled!

I applied to a special high school program at the local college in Cupertino. I was accepted into this college and spent my senior year at De Anza College, where I had some fantastic teachers who became mentors and role models. I then wrestled for Menlo College for one year, and had the opportunity to compete on national television for WWE's $1,000,000 Tough Enough Championship on Smackdown. This competition began with over 10,000 entries and involved weekly eliminations, so needless to say, I was very excited and proud to have won such a dynamic show. Then, after a year of wrestling for the WWE, I was able to make a good name for myself and go back into the professional fighting world.

My point in all of this is to show you where I started and how far I've come. In my life, I found that when I was not focused and did not have a game plan for where I wanted my future to go, I was not able to fully commit to reaching my goals. Once I began to receive support and created a plan for my life, I started to succeed in all aspects of my life. I encourage you to set your eyes on your future and get excited to make goals for yourself. It will be these goals that will keep you focused and on the right path to achieving a successful future for yourself!

INSTRUCTIONS

In this lesson, I want you to start thinking about things in your life that motivate you. The goal is to focus on what you like and dislike. Understand that not everything that you like in life will be a benefit to you in the long run. For example, if you enjoy sleeping in on a school day, this will not help your chances for success because being on time to school and being in attendance to all of your classes will allow you to get the most out of your education. Now, think about some of the things in your life that you dislike. For example, if you dislike doing homework, it is important to acknowledge that doing your homework will help you to achieve good grades and, in turn, will help lead you to graduation, which is a step in the right direction for success. Therefore, when going through this chapter, I want you to keep in mind that even though you may like something, it may not be beneficial for you. The same goes for things in your life that you dislike. There may be things that you really don't enjoy doing, but if you can find something positive in those things that you can use to benefit you and your future, you will go a long way in life! The key to being successful is to learn how to transform both your likes and dislikes into habits that are important to your future success.

On the following lines, write down what you like according to each topic and then next to that, write down the reason why you like it.

School

1. _____,_____

2. _____,_____

3. _____,_____

4. _____,_____

How does school help you succeed?

_____

_____

Sports/Fitness/Health

1. _____,_____

2. _____,_____

3. _____,_____

4. _____,_____

How do sports/fitness/health help you succeed?

_____

_____

Arts (i.e. music, drawing, poetry)

1. _____,_____

2. _____,_____

3. _____,_____

4. _____,_____

How does art help you succeed?

_____

_____

Hobbies/Activities

1. _____,_____

2. _____,_____

3. _____,_____

4. _____,_____

How do hobbies/activities help you succeed?

_____

_____

Family

1. _____,_____
2. _____,_____
3. _____,_____
4. _____,_____

How does your family help you succeed?

_____

_____

Places you would like visit

1. _____,_____
2. _____,_____
3. _____,_____
4. _____,_____

Friends

1. _____,_____
2. _____,_____
3. _____,_____
4. _____,_____

How do your friends help you succeed?

_____

_____

Work (i.e. household chores, employment)

1. _____,_____
2. _____,_____
3. _____,_____

DANIEL PUDER

4. _____,_____

What kind of job do you want to have?

_____

_____

What other things do you like that are not mentioned above? Why?

1. _____,_____
2. _____,_____
3. _____,_____
4. _____,_____

Now rank your top nine likes (one from each section above):

1. _____
2. _____
3. _____
4. _____
5. _____
6. _____
7. _____
8. _____
9. _____

Now, continue the same as above; however, this time, write down what you dislike according to each topic and then next to that, write down the reason why you dislike it.

School

1. _____,_____
2. _____,_____
3. _____,_____
4. _____,_____

How do these dislikes affect your grades?

_____

_____

Sports/Fitness/Health

1. _____,_____
2. _____,_____
3. _____,_____
4. _____,_____

How do these dislikes affect your life?

_____

_____

Arts (i.e. music, drawing, poetry)

1. _____,_____
2. _____,_____
3. _____,_____
4. _____,_____

How do these dislikes affect your life?

_____

_____

Hobbies/Activities

1. _____,_____
2. _____,_____
3. _____,_____
4. _____,_____

How do these dislikes affect your life?

_____

_____

Family

1. _____,_____
2. _____,_____
3. _____,_____
4. _____,_____

How do these dislikes affect your life?

_____

_____

Friends

1. _____,_____
2. _____,_____
3. _____,_____
4. _____,_____

How do these dislikes affect your relationships with friends?

_____

_____

Work (i.e. household chores, employment)

1. _____,_____
2. _____,_____
3. _____,_____
4. _____,_____

How do these dislikes affect your life?

_____

_____

What other things do you dislike that are not mentioned above? Why?

1. _____,_____
2. _____,_____
3. _____,_____
4. _____,_____

Now rank your top eight dislikes (one from each section above):

1._____
2. _____
3. _____
4. _____
5. _____
6. _____
7. _____
8. _____

Until you get to Chapter 2, take time every day to write down more things that you like or dislike. This will help you understand yourself better. By learning more about what makes you happy, you'll be able to make the best choices for your life.

"I believe that we each hold a responsibility to share our knowledge and help those that follow to be able to learn from our experiences. The easy road in life is to follow others. But the best life is one when we help others and stand up for each other, get involved, and take action. This is where greatness lives."

— Boe Trumbull, Senior Director of Operations, Logistics, and Special Projects, SBE Entertainment Group

DANIEL PUDER

CHAPTER 2
FIND A MENTOR
by Daniel Puder

There are many benefits to having mentors in your life. Mentors are there for you and can be a sounding board for your ideas as well as your obstacles. They can draw upon their own experiences—both their successes and their failures—to help you make the right decisions in life. They can help you network with other people to further yourself socially and professionally. Most important, they are individuals who you can trust.

Here are a few of the mentors who have changed my life:

My parents

My parents have given me tremendous support and direction over the years. When I was four years old, they helped me start my first business by purchasing chickens for me so that I could sell the eggs to my neighbors. My dad has been a great influence to me as he has an MBA, and is president/CEO of his own company. He often gives me advice in business projects and has guided me through life. My mother taught me to always treat women with respect and that a little thoughtful gift, like buying a girl flowers, goes a long way. While growing up, they supported me through thick and thin, and for that, I love them.

Harlan and Madeline Gittin

Harlan and Madelin Gittin have been my second family in Los Angeles. I've spent a lot of time with them and they've given me a lot of direction in my life. Not only have they helped keep me grounded, they've also taught me to always remember what is most important in life. Harlan constantly reminds me of "friends and friendlies," which means you should never have an enemy. It's not a good idea to have people angry with you, because you never know if you'll run into them in the future. Imagine if the kid you teased in grade school grew up to own the company you wanted to work for as an adult. The world is a small place and you never want to burn bridges.

Ed Conners

I met Ed Connors when I was 22 years old, which was before I made a name for myself with mixed martial arts and pro-wrestling. One day when

I was in southern California with some friends, they introduced me to Ed and ever since then, he has been a friend and a mentor to me. When I met Ed for the first time, he asked me what I wanted out of life and I told him I wanted to be a professional athlete. He offered me the following advice: 1) Get in shape (physically and mentally), 2) Bleach my hair (this would help me to stand out from other individuals in this industry), and 3) Get a tan. Guess what, he was right! Just following his three simple suggestions set me apart from the other fighters and wrestlers at that time. Above all, the thing that most impressed me about Ed was his genuine desire to help others succeed. He has housed over six hundred athletes in order to help them be able to pursue their athletic careers when finances were tough, and he also paid for other expenses including food, gym fees, clothing, and dietary supplements. Overall, Ed is an amazing man and has been a mentor to many athletes.

Dave Meltzer

Dave is one of the top MMA and pro-wrestling writers in the world. He has been a blessing in my life and has directed me throughout my career. When I was in the WWE, I would be on the phone with him for hours each week. He would give me advice and inspiration—and still does today!

Boe Trumbull

I met Boe when I moved to Hollywood. He's an executive at a large entertainment company. There's a big difference between living in Northern California and Hollywood. Hollywood is much faster paced, as everyone moves here from all over the world to become the next star. Boe guided me to make the right decisions for my future and helped me steer clear of things that could have led me down the wrong path.

Todd Burns

I met Todd in the early 2000's when he was studying at Pepperdine University for his JD/MBA. Todd is not only one of the smartest people I know, he's also one of the hardest workers in the world! He now owns a few companies in Los Angeles, but what makes Todd stand out in Los Angeles are his morals. Thanks to Todd, I've been in Hollywood for over three years and I have not compromised my morals once.

Mr. Star

When I was in second grade, I had a fantastic teacher, Mr. Star, who taught me something I'll never forget. On his birthday, he brought cookies for the whole class. Since I was that kid who loved sweets, I asked him for a second cookie and he said, "No." I looked at Mr. Star, confused, and asked, "Why not?" He replied, "You didn't say thank you for the first cookie." I was not very happy about this at the time, but it taught me one of life's biggest lessons. **(You should not only tell others "thank you" when they do something for you or give you something, but you should also be thankful for what you have every day of your life.)**

Along with the people mentioned above, there are many more who have made a difference in my life. I want to thank everyone who has helped me get where I am today. This is a team effort and I'm glad to be in the mix!

What are 10 qualities that you look for in a mentor? (Good morals, successful career, educated, honest, punctual, etc.)

1._____ 2._____
3._____ 4._____
5._____ 6._____
7._____ 8._____
9._____ 10._____

The qualities that you listed should be positive qualities that you will strive to possess in your own life while you work toward achieving success. Now I want you to sign the line below stating that you are dedicated to working hard to incorporate these above qualities into your own life:

Name:_____Sign:_____Date:_____

A mentor is someone who becomes a part of your life and helps guide you as you make decisions that will lead you to be successful. A mentor is someone who truly cares about you and your well-being and has the time and ability to help you reach your full potential. You can find a mentor throughout your life in many places in your community. Anyone can be a mentor, as long as they possess the qualities that you are seeking. Remember, having a mentor is extremely helpful with reaching success. Don't be afraid to ask someone to be your mentor. There are many people who would be willing and honored to take on this important role in your life.

Today, you are taking a stand to improve your life by finding a mentor. You just took a HUGE first step. By saying that you want to have a great life and that you are ready to work toward this goal with all your fellow My Life My Power members.

Who would be a good mentor for you? Why?

1. _____, _____
2. _____,_____
3. _____,_____
4. _____,_____

Now, ask each one of the above individuals to be your mentor.

What are some questions that you have for your mentors?

1. _____

2. _____

3. _____

4. _____

What positive advice have they given to you that you have used in the past?

1. _____

2. _____

3. _____

4. _____

I have sometimes thought, "Wow, this person would be a GREAT mentor," and then it turns out that they don't truly possess the qualities that I look for in someone I call a mentor. If this happens to you, keep looking and don't be discouraged. It could take some time to find even just a few quality mentors that you can depend on, but it's worth it.

The next step after finding a mentor is to spend time around the type of people that you admire. Have you ever heard the saying, "guilty by association", this means that if you surround yourself with negative people you will be linked to their negative actions and the negative stigma that they carry. On the other hand, there's another saying that says "success breeds success". This means, if you surround yourself with positive-minded, successful people you will open up more opportunities to succeed. One thing to remember is to stay true to who you are and never compromise your values to gain an advantage.

The last exercise of this chapter is to look back on a time or times when you were given bad advice by someone that you looked up to. By writing down and understanding these experiences, you can learn that not all advice is good advice. That is why having a good quality mentor is important.

Write down some bad advice you received and briefly explain what made it bad advice.

1. _____

_____

2. _____

_____

3. _____

_____

4. _____

_____

Finding a mentor in life is one of the smartest things you can do. Best of all, you're never too young or too old to find a mentor or to be a mentor yourself. Once you have the right mentor, be sure to listen to their advice and ask questions. Mentors will help you learn from their mistakes and keep you on the right path. Think about it. Older and wiser people can guide you away from making the same mistakes they made, which will allow you to achieve your goals much faster.

DP's quote: **"It's all about friends and friendlies."** – from Harlan Gittin

"When confronting your fears, keep your sight set on your end goal and know that you can work through it!"

— Niv Ashkenazi, Classical Violinist

CHAPTER 3
CONFRONT YOUR FEARS

by Daniel Puder

About five days before one of my first MMA fights, my brother David called and asked how I was handling the pressure.

David was a Division 1 National Rowing Champion for Cal Berkeley and has undergone a lot of mental training, just like myself. I told him, "The only thing I'm scared of is losing."

He said, "Why don't you reverse that fear."

Confused, I asked, "What do you mean?"

He explained, "You have trained with the top fighters in the world, so you should be confident in knowing that you have prepared yourself to the best of your ability. Enjoying what you do in life is better than going through life with unnecessary stress and pressure."

It was like a light turned on in my head. At that moment, I changed my out-look on how I was going to adjust my thoughts about my fights. By taking my brother's advice, I was able to overcome a huge fear, and I have since applied that advice to include all of my personal and professional challenges. Whether you're studying for a test, competing in a sport, or applying for a job, it's important to focus on doing your best rather than being preoccupied with a negative outcome.

What do you fear? When you wake up in the morning and you open your eyes, what are your first thoughts? For me, I think it is going to be another perfect day. However, for many people that I've helped, they think, "Oh, no! I have to go to school and deal with these bullies." The goal of this lesson is to help you understand your fears so that you can overcome them. Then you'll have a much more enjoyable life. Remember, truly experiencing every-thing life has to offer is a good thing. This includes experiencing the feelings of fear, frustration, happiness, love, and all of the other emotions a person can feel. This makes you a more complete and well-rounded person.

What are your greatest fears? (i.e. Failure, not fitting in, disappointing your family or friends, rejection, not having enough time to do everything, being misunderstood by your peers, supporting yourself financially)

1._____ 2._____
3._____ 4._____
5._____ 6._____
7._____ 8._____

What negative consequences have these fears caused you in the past? (i.e. Are you giving up? Are you feeling rejected? Do you feel stressed out?)

1._____
2._____
3._____
4._____
5._____
6._____

How have these fears held you back?

1._____
2._____
3._____
4._____
5._____
6._____

What would happen if you got rid of your fears now?

1._____
2._____
3._____
4._____
5._____
6._____

How are you going to do this and how long will it take? It depends on the person and the experience. Let me tell you, when I was younger, I did not like reading in front of people because I was a slow reader. Because of that, until high school, I did everything I could to avoid reading aloud in class. Years later, I learned that if I'm not very good at something, like reading, it helped to just say the following to my audience before I start:

"I am very good at my sport, but I am a little slow at reading, so bear with me."

Breaking the ice beforehand allows you to take the focus away from being nervous and gets a good laugh out of your audience. Trust me, people will respect you for this.

Which mentors or peers are you going to ask for help confronting your fears? Why would you ask these mentors?

1. _____
2. _____
3. _____
4. _____
5. _____
6. _____

Think about all of your fears. You need to make the decision right now to get rid of them. Fewer fears and less stress will enable you to work harder and perform better, allowing you to get what you want out of life. In the upcoming lessons, I'll teach you how to manage fears and eventually get rid of them.

DP's quote: **"Why fear life when you can love life?"**

"At some point every leader will experience failure. However, a successful leader doesn't let that failure ruin them. The quality that distinguishes winning leaders from the rest of them is their ability to handle the inevitable failures and mistakes that are a part of the human condition with grace and truth."

— Lindsay Sullivan, Pro tennis player, Leadership Development Specialist

CHAPTER 4

LEARN FROM YOUR SUCCESSES AND FAILURES

by Daniel Puder

When I was a kid, school was the only thing that I didn't excel in. Even once I became a professional fighter, I experienced failure—even though I've never lost a fight. During my first pro fight in Japan, I repeatedly tried the same key-lock move on my opponent and it didn't work at all. I finally won by changing my approach. After the fight, my coaches told me what I did wrong, and from there, I never made that same mistake again. I knew I almost lost the fight by continuing to make the same mistake.

Throughout my life, I've tried to listen to good advice and learn from others' successes and failures. Failing made me work harder and smarter the second time around. Most importantly, I've learned to never give up on myself no matter how bad things get. There have been times when things weren't going as planned, but I always remembered to keep pushing forward—even if that meant initially taking a step or two back—because I knew that is how I would be successful.

Everybody fails at some point in their life. Everyone makes mistakes. The important thing is to be able to learn from them so that you can avoid repeating the same mistakes.

It's not only important to learn from your failures; you also want to learn from your successes. Rather than just relishing your successes, you should look back and analyze what you did right so you can replicate it the next time. You should also take note of anything you could have done better. This will help you get further faster and will increase your chances of success in the future.

I consider one of my greatest successes to be the way I've learned to treat people. I definitely believe that if you do good things for others, good things will flow back to you naturally. Conversely, if you do bad things, it can lead to one frustration after another. It's not about being perfect, but about trying hard to be the best person you can be.

Before we go further, let me tell you a few things I've seen my childhood friends do that have really made their lives harder: fighting in the streets, drinking and driving, doing drugs, or getting into trouble. All of these decisions put them on difficult paths and have delayed them from achieving their goals. If you feel like you have fallen into these traps, it is never too late to turn your life around.

List five times that you have failed. Why do you think this happened?

1. _____, _____
2. _____, _____
3. _____, _____
4. _____, _____
5. _____, _____

Understand that the key to success is learning from each failure and thinking about what you could have done differently.

For the five failures that you wrote about, what have you learned from each of them?

1. _____
2. _____
3. _____
4. _____
5. _____

You and I need to have the same goal in this process, which is to help you succeed. The following questions are about your successes. I believe that you can learn just as much from success as you can from failure.

List your five greatest successes.

1. _____
2. _____
3. _____
4. _____
5. _____

DANIEL PUDER

What did you learn from each of these five successes?

1. _____

2. _____

3. _____

4. _____

5. _____

Now, I will provide you with three actions steps. These steps are for you to learn from your successes and failures:

1. When you fail at something, you must understand the reason for this failure and take note of what you can do differently the next time.

2. When you succeed, learn what you did right and take note of ways that you can improve the next time.

3. Spend less time around negative people, and more time with positive people. Everyone that you encounter in life can teach you something. Learn from others' successes and failures and you will achieve your goals faster and you will be happier.

DP's quotes: **"Failures are simply opportunities to sharpen your skills."**

"There is no such thing as a failure unless you don't try."

"One key to success: never let your fears take control of you. Instead, let your fears motivate you to perform at your highest level in everything you do."

— Kyle "Kingsbu" Kingsbury, Ultimate Fighting Championships (UFC) Light Heavyweight Fighter, Spike TV's "The Ultimate Fighter Season 8: Team Nogueira vs. Team Mir"

CHAPTER 5

ANALYZE YOUR PRODUCTIVITY

by Daniel Puder

People always ask me how I am able to juggle all the work I do. As you know, I wear many hats: undefeated MMA fighter, Director of Youth Programs for CUshop.org, and founder of My Life My Power. Each of these jobs requires a tremendous amount of time and commitment, but I'm able to succeed in all of them and still have time for a healthy social life because of my efficient time management skills.

What's the best use of your time right now? The following assessment will show you how much time you're spending on the things that will make you successful in life versus the things that will keep you from being successful both now and in the future. The best use of your time isn't always being productive in terms of school or sports. Sometimes, productivity means spending quality time with your family and friends, enjoying nature, reading a book, or learning a new hobby or skill. The key to life is being well-rounded.

Roughly how many hours a day do you spend on the following activities?

HOURS PER DAY:

Productive Activities

Studying/homework:	½ - 1 - 2 - 3 - 4 - 5 - 6
Do your parents ask you to do chores?	YES NO
If yes, do you willingly help?	YES NO
Chores:	½ - 1 - 2 - 3 - 4 - 5 - 6
Physical activity/sports:	½ - 1 - 2 - 3 - 4 - 5 - 6
Hobbies/skills:	½ - 1 - 2 - 3 - 4 - 5 - 6
Spending time with Your family:	½ - 1 - 2 - 3 - 4 - 5 - 6

Distractions

Television:	½ - 1 - 2 - 3 - 4 - 5 - 6
Video games:	½ - 1 - 2 - 3 - 4 - 5 - 6

| Internet: | ½ - 1 - 2 - 3 - 4 - 5 - 6 |
| Talking on the phone or texting: | ½ - 1 - 2 - 3 - 4 - 5 - 6 |

How many text messages do you send per day? _____

You need a mixture of productive activities and distractions. The goal is to have a well-rounded life, but you need to take care of your responsibilities done before you can go have fun! Work before play! Understanding this distinction can help you juggle competing demands on your time.

One of my rules in life is to get what you need done before the fun! The reason for this is that once you finish what you absolutely have to do, you don't have any stress, you aren't worried about finishing, and you can go play, have fun and really enjoy life.

Let me give you an example: I was speaking with a group of high school students in Los Angeles about this concept and one of them told me that he always has fun and doesn't care about his homework or other responsibilities. I asked him to refer back to where he wrote down in his book the qualities that he looks for in a mentor. I then asked him to read his list of mentor qualities to the other students. *His top five qualities were as follows: fun, helpful, honest, responsible, and punctual.*

After hearing what his list included, I asked him if he thought that he should possess those same qualities. If so, would he be willing to make the change needed to do so? He thought about it for a minute, and said that he agreed and knew he needed to make a change. My next question was when he would make a change, to which he responded, "I don't know." I asked him, "How fast can you make a change?" With a puzzled look on his face, he said, "Fast."

I said, "OK, well, do you want to make a commitment today to your friends in this group and change right now?" His response: "I will!"

Below, you will see a line on which, today, you will make a commitment to make sure your work and responsibilities are done before you have fun. You are making this commitment to all of your parents, friends, mentors, peers, and most importantly, to yourself.

Name:_____Sign:_____ Date:_____

Now get ten of your friends and teachers to initial this, which will show that they know you are committed and will hold you to it.

_____, _____, _____, _____, _____

_____, _____, _____, _____, _____

In your daily schedule at the end of the book, be sure to check the box for each day that you complete your responsibilities before having fun.

Out of all of your productive activities and distractions, list the top five things you need to do on a daily basis to reach your goals in life:

1. _____

2. _____

3. _____

4. _____

5. _____

Before you move on to Chapter 6, make sure that you have completed all of the previous chapter work. If yes, GREAT! Move ahead to the next chapter. If not, please go back and complete the chapter work. If you are having trouble with anything in these chapters, ask your mentors or a peer for help. To be able to get the most out of the My Life My Power program, it is important to be thorough and complete all assignments.

DP's quote: **"Be responsible and reliable first, then enjoy your free time."**

"My Life My Power is the type of program that will have a real impact. Involving the right people and enabling youths to help youths is what separates this program from other failed programs. Daniel Puder is a dynamo and will be a driving force to the success of this program."

— Sergeant Bobby Lopez, San Jose Police Department, President of the Fraternal Order of Police Lodge 52

CHAPTER 6

ESTABLISH YOUR GOALS

by Daniel Puder

When I was younger, I didn't set goals. I didn't have a program like My Life My Power to help guide me. I just wanted to make it through life. It wasn't until high school that I learned to set goals for myself. My first goals were to become a top wrestler, graduate high school, and somehow make it into college (all of which I am proud to say that I successfully accomplished). Once I got into college, I concentrated on earning a degree and learning as much as possible. I also had visions of becoming an elite college wrestler and starting my own company.

During my senior year in college, I was given an opportunity to compete in a potentially life-changing competition for World Wrestling Entertainment. This led me to not only create new long-term goals but to set short-term goals along the way. In order to achieve long-term success, I needed to train harder and work harder than anyone else in the competition. I also needed to practice my speaking promos so that I could perform better on television. I figured that if I put a game plan together and worked harder than anyone else, I could win the WWE contract, and at the end of the six-week competition, I had the most online fan votes and went on to become the Million Dollar Tough Enough Champion.

A couple years after the WWE victory, I fought in mixed martial arts events for Bodog Fights. They had an online competition for a $15,000 prize, so I put together an online marketing and self-promotion plan to win. My hard work paid off, because I smashed the online competition and won every category possible. What I've learned time and time again is that if I have a game plan and put in 100% effort, I can accomplish anything.

Do you want a good job? Yes   No

When do you want to get a job or internship?

Now   1 year   2 years   3 years   Other _____

Refer to your resume tips chapter and build your personal resume.

What do want to do when you graduate? _____

_____

How much money do you want to make? _____

Now, turn to the Money 101: Staying Financially Fit chapter. I want for you to write down how much you want to make per year, as well as fill in all of the budgeting information.

When do you want to move out of your family's home? _____
_____

Where do you see yourself living? _____
_____

Do you see yourself having pets?   Yes   No   Maybe

What kind of pets? _____

(Rate the following questions based upon your relationships with others)

How do you treat people?   Poorly   Well   Very Well

How do they treat you?   Poorly   Well   Very Well

Do you see yourself getting married? Yes   No   Maybe

Do you see yourself having kids? Yes   No

What do you want to be know for? _____
_____

What are the top six things that you currently dislike (refer to Chapter 1, Discover Your Passions).

     1._____ 2._____
     3._____ 4._____
     5._____ 6._____

Write down what you could do for each of those six things to make them more enjoyable. For instance, if you don't like homework, you could create a study group with your friends or get a tutor to help you so that you can understand your school work.

1._____
_____

2. _____

   _____

3. _____

   _____

4. _____

   _____

5. _____

   _____

6. _____

   _____

Now that you have established your goals and what you hope to get out of your life, you will be able to move onto the next chapter where you will be asked to set a time line for yourself in order to successfully achieve these goals.

DP's quote: **"Set a plan, surround yourself with smart and successful people, and you will succeed."**

"My Life My Power is a well-organized, thoughtful, and easy-to-follow trail map for youth who want to learn how to become the best version of themselves."

—Amin Nikfar, M.Ed., Olympian (shot put), Iranian National Record Holder, Iranian National Champion

CHAPTER 7
SET A TIMELINE
by Daniel Puder

When I finally began to turn my life around, I sat down and listed out my goals and then created a game plan for how I was going to achieve them. I needed more than a goal—I needed direction.

A goal without a plan is simply a wish. You need to divide your goals into short-term, mid-range, and long-term goals. These goals should be dynamic, meaning that they aren't set in stone and can be adjusted if necessary. You don't need to put pressure on yourself to have all the answers right now. The important thing is to always be progressing and thinking forward about how you can better yourself. Time lines will help you achieve your goals.

The following exercise will allow you to set some short-term goals for yourself. Make sure to pay close attention as I have listed your goals starting at 1 month, then 10 year, 4 year, 1 year, 6 month, and 3 month. The reason for this is because I want for you to first establish your goals for the next month, then be able to think long term in order to achieve those goals and from there, work backwards with your time line.

1-Month Goals

School/Work:

1._____ 2._____
3._____ 4._____
5._____ 6._____

Personal:

1._____ 2._____
3._____ 4._____
5._____ 6._____

Friends:

1._____ 2._____

3._____ 4._____
5._____ 6._____

Family:

1._____ 2._____
3._____ 4._____
5._____ 6._____

Health/Fitness:

1._____ 2._____
3._____ 4._____
5._____ 6._____

Fun/Travel:

1._____ 2._____
3._____ 4._____
5._____ 6._____

Other:
1._____ 2._____
3._____ 4._____
5._____ 6._____

Long-term and Lifetime Goals
10-Year and Longer Goals

School/Work:

1._____ 2._____
3._____ 4._____
5._____ 6._____

Personal:

1._____ 2._____
3._____ 4._____
5._____ 6._____

Friends:

1._____ 2._____
3._____ 4._____
5._____ 6._____

Family:

1._____ 2._____
3._____ 4._____
5._____ 6._____

Health/Fitness:

1._____ 2._____
3._____ 4._____
5._____ 6._____

Fun/Travel:

1._____ 2._____
3._____ 4._____
5._____ 6._____

Other:

1._____ 2._____
3._____ 4._____
5._____ 6._____

4-Year Goals

School/Work:

1._____ 2._____
3._____ 4._____
5._____ 6._____

Personal:

1._____ 2._____
3._____ 4._____

5._____ 6._____

Friends:

1._____ 2._____
3._____ 4._____
5._____ 6._____

Family:

1._____ 2._____
3._____ 4._____
5._____ 6._____

Health/Fitness:

1._____ 2._____
3._____ 4._____
5._____ 6._____

Fun/Travel:

1._____ 2._____
3._____ 4._____
5._____ 6._____

Other:

1._____ 2._____
3._____ 4._____
5._____ 6._____

Mid-range

1-Year Goals

School/Work:

1._____ 2._____
3._____ 4._____
5._____ 6._____

Personal:

1._____ 2._____
3._____ 4._____
5._____ 6._____

Friends:

1._____ 2._____
3._____ 4._____
5._____ 6._____

Family:

1._____ 2._____
3._____ 4._____
5._____ 6._____

Health/Fitness:

1._____ 2._____
3._____ 4._____
5._____ 6._____

Fun/Travel:

1._____ 2._____
3._____ 4._____
5._____ 6._____

Other:

1._____ 2._____
3._____ 4._____
5._____ 6._____

6-Month Goals

School/Work:

1._____ 2._____
3._____ 4._____
5._____ 6._____

Personal:

1._____ 2._____
3._____ 4._____
5._____ 6._____

Friends:

1._____ 2._____
3._____ 4._____
5._____ 6._____

Family:

1._____ 2._____
3._____ 4._____
5._____ 6._____

Health/Fitness:

1._____ 2._____
3._____ 4._____
5._____ 6._____

Fun/Travel:

1._____ 2._____
3._____ 4._____
5._____ 6._____

Other:

1._____ 2._____
3._____ 4._____
5._____ 6._____

3-Month Goals

School/Work:

1._____ 2._____
3._____ 4._____
5._____ 6._____

Personal:

1._____ 2._____
3._____ 4._____
5._____ 6._____

Friends:

1._____ 2._____
3._____ 4._____
5._____ 6._____

Family:

1._____ 2._____
3._____ 4._____
5._____ 6._____

Health/Fitness:

1._____ 2._____
3._____ 4._____
5._____ 6._____

Fun/Travel:

1._____ 2._____
3._____ 4._____
5._____ 6._____

Other:

1._____ 2._____
3._____ 4._____
5._____ 6._____

Pick a short-term (S), mid-term (M), and long-term (L) goal for each of the following so that you can begin this process today.

School/Work:

S._____
M._____
L._____

Personal:

S._____

M._____

L._____

Friends:

S._____

M._____

L._____

Family:

S._____

M._____

L._____

Health/Fitness:

S._____

M._____

L._____

Fun/Travel:

S._____

M._____

L._____

Other:

S._____

M._____

L._____

Work on these goals for the next month and then revisit them. It's helpful to share your list with your mentors and support group. They can help you with the steps needed to achieve these goals. Remember, don't get thrown off if things change. Sometimes your path shifts and you need to change direction. It's perfectly OK to alter your goals at any time; however, only do so when necessary.

Now that you've selected the short-term and long-term goals you're going to work on, prioritize your daily tasks 1-7, with one being the first thing you are going do and seven being the last thing on your to-do list.

School/Work: _____

Personal: _____

Friends: _____

Family: _____

Health/Fitness: _____

Fun/Travel: _____

Other: _____

Time is always a limiting factor, which is why it's important to complete your most important obligations first. My advice is to use the My Life My Power daily planner located in the back of the book. This will allow you to write down your top priorities for each day and make sure you complete your tasks.

DP's quote: **"While your goals may change, make sure you always have long-term vision."**

"Health and happiness are beyond the physical. They're a point of view and mental attitudes you have about yourself, your life, and your relationships."

— Tina Morse, Life Doctor, MA, MFT

CHAPTER 8

CREATE YOUR WELLNESS VISION

by Tina Morse

What areas of health and well-being do you want to improve upon?

1._____   2._____
3._____   4._____
5._____   6._____

What are some strengths that you already possess?

1._____   2._____
3._____   4._____
5._____   6._____

What are one or more qualities that you would like to have in your life?

Note: It can be a quality that you believe is missing or something that you admire about someone else. Some examples include patience, dedication, wisdom, etc.

1._____   2._____
3._____   4._____
5._____   6._____

Imagine that you possess all of these qualities. How does it feel?

_____
_____
_____
_____
_____

After you imagine this, I want you to initial here: _____

Write a statement about these qualities already being a part of who you are. Begin with "I am."

Note: This will help ground you in your quality. For example, if your quality is love you could write: "I am love, and I experience that I am loved through the way I continually care for myself physically, mentally, emotionally, and spiritually. I am love, and you can see me reflected through the kind words I use and the support I continually share."

_____

_____

_____

_____

_____

PHYSICALLY

I am nurturing and caring for myself physically by:

Examples: "Setting boundaries that physically support me. My home and school environments and the people around me support me and reflect who I am." "Surrounding myself with healthy people who show they care and I learn, grow and am inspired by them." "Eating food that is natural and un-processed, healthy, and delicious." "Making sure I get some form of exercise or physical activity daily so that I can be strong and healthy."

_____

_____

_____

_____

MENTALLY

I am nurturing and caring for myself mentally by:

Examples: "Reading something positive as soon as I get up because that helps me start my day on a good note." "Focusing on the positive throughout my day and taking a giant eraser to any negative thoughts." "Immediately replacing negative thoughts with positive ones." "Journaling about something I'm grateful for right before I go to sleep."

_____

_____

_____

_____

EMOTIONALLY

I am nurturing and caring for myself emotionally by:

Examples: "Creating something wonderful and handmade for my best friend's birthday. It feels good to reflect on how much someone means to me by making them a gift with my own two hands." "Engaging in life with passion and purpose, which makes me feel alive and excited about my day."

_____

_____

_____

_____

SPIRITUALLY

I am nurturing and caring for myself spiritually by:

Examples: "Listening to or reading inspirational messages that I can learn and grow from as well as feel supported and connected." "Watching films that touch me with their meaning and message."

_____

_____

_____

_____

What is one action in each of the categories listed above that you would be willing to make time for each day no matter what?

_____

_____

_____

_____

_____

Note: Making life changes takes time. Think baby steps to ensure a positive experience. Simply writing down your steps will be your first move toward making a change.

"I have always placed a great importance on creating opportunities for others so they may also have the chance to excel in life no matter where they came from. I would like to see my work colleagues and their families pursue their goals and dreams through higher education combined with strong character and values. I hope that I can use the combination of my personal and professional life experiences to further the work of the Los Angeles School Police Department (LASPD) and provide a foundation on which my colleagues can succeed."

— Detective Rudy Perez, Los Angeles School Police Department,
Co-Founder of Friends of Safe Schools Los Angeles

Chapter 9

RESTORATIVE PRACTICES

by James Ream, Brittney Lozano, and Daniel Puder

If you are unfamiliar with the term restorative practices, you are probably wondering what it means and how it relates to you. In simple terms, restorative practices shows you how to take responsibility for your actions, build and maintain healthy relationships, and learn how to respect others through a few simple steps. It is impossible for any of us to be perfect or have perfect relationships with others. However, it is possible to realize when a poor decision has been made that has hurt others and immediately do something about it. Fix it, repair it, restore it, and learn from it!

A zero-tolerance policy can be a disciplinary action and/or immediate suspension from school when a student gets in trouble for certain offenses. Restorative practices were created in contrast to the zero-tolerance policy. They allow everyone who was involved in a situation to discuss how they can make the situation right. They allow you to openly share your feelings, build and maintain healthy relationships, and learn how to work through problems and challenges, as well as teach you how to hold yourself accountable for the things that you say and do. While the hurt and pain that an incident causes to those involved cannot be taken back, talking through things truly can be a healing process for everyone. Most importantly, the restorative practices approach gets you thinking outside of yourself. You will realize that every decision and action you make causes either a negative or positive reaction in others. Therefore, as a result of every decision that you make, good or bad, someone else is affected in some way—it could be your friends, family, teachers, or even a complete stranger.

I would like you to answer the following questions as truthfully as possible. Take some time to think before you answer. For the last two questions, fill in the blanks with individuals that you have a relationship with and answer accordingly.

I would rank my relationship with my PARENTS as:
very good   good   not so good

I would rank my relationship with my SIBLINGS as:
very good   good   not so good

I would rank my relationship with my FRIENDS as:

very good   good   not so good

I would rank my relationship with my TEACHERS as:

very good   good   not so good

I would rank my relationship with my _____ as:

very good   good   not so good

I would rank my relationship with my _____ as:

very good   good   not so good

Have you ever stopped to think about what a healthy relationship means to you? I would like you to write down some positive qualities that you think define a healthy relationship (i.e. honesty, trust, respect, etc.).

1. _____   2. _____

3. _____   4. _____

5. _____   6. _____

Now that you have determined some of the qualities that you look for within a healthy relationship, let's discuss how restorative practices can help you to maintain those healthy relationships. No matter what type of situation you are in, following the basic guidelines that restorative practices teaches will allow you to become happier, more confident, and more focused in all areas of your life. Now, you might be thinking to yourself, "I doubt that following a simple process could really help me in my life and in my relationships." If you are the person questioning how effective it really can be, just give it a try and see what you think.

In order for you to be able to get the most out of the restorative practices approach, I have provided some simple steps to get you prepared for addressing an incident. Once you have completed these steps, use the questions as a guideline for your discussion with everyone involved.

Steps for Restorative Practices:
1. Ask yourself what harm was done.
2. Ask yourself who was harmed. Then put together a list of everyone who was involved and invite them to be part of the discussion to address the incident.
3. Find an adult who can be present during the discussion.

4. Remember to keep an open mind and be willing to hear everyone's perspective of the incident.

The questions below are ones that you can use during your discussion with everyone present. By going through these questions together, it will allow everyone an equal opportunity to listen and talk about their feelings in order to develop and maintain healthy relationships.

The next time you find yourself dealing with a situation that has negatively affected someone else, I urge you to refer back to the steps above and use these questions to work through the situation. In order for you to have a better understanding of how to use these questions in the future, I want you to think back to a time when you either got in trouble for making a bad decision or a time when you made a bad decision that you should have gotten in trouble for. Now, walk yourself through these questions and remember to answer them honestly.

If you were the one that caused harm to someone else, these are the questions that you would ask yourself:

Briefly explain what happened.

_____
_____
_____
_____

While the incident was happening, what were you thinking about?

_____
_____
_____

Since the incident, what additional thoughts have you had?

_____
_____
_____

Who was affected by your actions? HOW were they affected?

_____
_____
_____
_____

In order to make what happened right, what do you think you must do?

_____
_____

_____

_____

_____

If you were the person that was harmed by someone else's behavior, these are the questions that you would use:

How did you feel and what did you think after the incident occurred?

_____

_____

_____

_____

What type of impact has this incident had on you and those around you?

_____

_____

_____

_____

What was the most difficult part of getting through this incident for you?

_____

_____

_____

_____

What do you think should happen in order for this incident to be made right?

_____

_____

_____

_____

Let's take bullying for example. I think that we can all agree that bullying is wrong and that no one should be made fun of or physically abused for any reason. When you begin the bullying chapter in this book, you will learn that there are typically three sets of people involved: the bully, the person being bullied, and the witness to the bullying, called a bystander. When a bullying incident occurs, it can make the bully feel empowered by belittling someone else, it can make the person being bullied feel lonely and depressed, and it can make the bystander feel helpless and scared. Through restorative practices, it is encouraged for everyone involved to come together, **preferably with the supervision of an adult,** and to openly answer and discuss the previously outlined questions. No matter what role you may have played in the situation, if you can truly allow yourself to be open-minded and listen to what others have to say, you will be amazed at the positive results that can be achieved. For the person who was being bullied, restorative practices can

DANIEL PUDER

help them regain a sense of empowerment because they are able to express to the bully how their treatment made them feel and why it caused so much pain. For the bully, it can allow them an opportunity to recognize what they are doing and even perhaps to understand why they choose to bully other people, and give them the knowledge as well as the power to make better decisions in the future.

I can guarantee that whenever a bad decision is made, someone is negatively affected. It is my hope that when you find yourself making a bad decision, you will think twice about your actions and behavior knowing that someone else may be hurt by it. If the situation occurs between you and a friend, use these questions to talk through things together. It will give you an opportunity to hear both sides of the story and to shift your perspective, mindset and understanding about how the other person feels. This is called empathy.

As we have discussed in previous chapters of this book, forming healthy relationships is important and maintaining these relationships is a key element to success and happiness. When you have friends to talk to, you are able to work through situations and express your feelings, thoughts, and emotions in a healthy way. If you face a situation where you may be having a disagreement with one of your friends, teachers, or family members, it is important to be able to talk through the situation with the person directly involved and strive to restore that relationship rather than letting it break down.

Sign on the line to make a pledge to work through conflicts by openly and honestly discussing the problem with all individuals involved, truly listening to their feelings and empathizing with those feelings.

Name:_____ Sign:_____Date:_____

"You will be amazed at how your life can change by putting the focus on helping others."

— Greg Collins, Actor, former NFL athlete

DANIEL PUDER

Chapter 10

CIVIC RESPONSIBILITY

by James Ream, Brittney Lozano, and Daniel Puder

When people who don't personally know me look at me, they think of Daniel Puder as a fighter and a pro wrestler. That is because this is what they have seen on TV, in magazines and in the media. However, my close friends and family have seen me for years giving back to different communities and charities. When I was young, my parents and I went to Mexico and helped build a house for people who were less fortunate. When I was in junior high, I spent my time working for Habitat for Humanity building a house for a family whose father has just been diagnosed with cancer, and whose small house was not sufficient for their five kids. Then, when I was nineteen years old, I realized that my passion was working with the youth and I started getting involved with a number of different charities to help kids. Now, I have started My Life My Power to be able to help kids like you.

As you read through this chapter, I urge you to think about what your passions are and come up with ways that you can use that passion to help others. One of the most fulfilling and rewarding things that you can do in your life is to give back. By "giving back," I am referring to volunteering your time and skills for a greater cause, which brings me to a term called "civic responsibility." In simple terms, civic responsibility involves the responsibilities that you have as a citizen. The great thing about civic responsibility it that you have the ability to use your talents, strengths, and passions to make a difference in your community and to those around you.

When you volunteer your time, you are not only helping others, you are helping yourself as well. To be successful in life, you must look beyond yourself and strive to make the community around you a better place. If you are planning to attend college and will be applying for college tuition grants, a history of volunteering is not only helpful, it is often required. When you volunteer, you will find new interests, meet new people, make new friends and begin to develop new perspectives on situations in life. Best of all, volunteering can be fun!

Let's face it, we all know the importance of lending a helping hand. Each of us has a civic responsibility to our friends, neighbors and community. Unfortunately, many times when it comes down to it, we get held back from helping or giving back. It doesn't have to be that way. Just choose to be a leader, choose to do your civic responsibility and get started.

Have you ever given up some of your time to be a volunteer?   Yes   No

If yes, what type of volunteer work did you do? _____

_____

_____

_____

Circle the types of volunteer work that you might be interested in.

1.   School clubs
2.   Student leadership
3.   Retirement homes
4.   Helping building a home, clinic, or school
5.   Mentoring children
6.   Working in after-school programs
7.   Teaching English as a second language
8.   Animal shelters
9.   Homeless shelters
10.   Trash cleanup/community beautification
11.   Children's hospitals
12.   Food bank/soup kitchen
13.   Helping a sibling with homework
14.   Other _____

Think for a moment about what you want people to say about you when you walk into a room. Do you want them to say that you are someone who is nice, generous, and helps others in need? You want people to respect you for what you stand for in life and for them to want you in their lives. Participating in extracurricular activities, having good grades, and helping out at the homeless shelter helps make you a well-rounded person. Wouldn't you agree?

Write down some things that you want others to say about you.

_____

_____

_____

_____

Personally, I want people to recognize the good that I bring to the community. I am by no means perfect and I have not been successful in everything I attempted. While I know that people will always associate me with being a professional fighter, I want them to also know me as someone who is now helping change the lives of millions of young people.

Here's something I want you to try: Take a stand in your own community or school and come up with ways that you can make a difference by looking beyond yourself and lending a hand to others.

What are some things that you and your friends could change for the better in your community or school?

_____

_____

_____

_____

Does your school have any students who have been bullied that you could help?   Yes   No

Are students littering your school with trash?   Yes   No

Does your school have any gangs?   Yes   No

Do you think that the people involved in the gangs could benefit from having something positive to belong to and be part of?   Yes   No

Is there a disabled student who could use help carrying their books between classes or could just use a friend to talk to?   Yes   No

Can you identify any other issues in your school that could use some improvement?   Yes   No

Name some other issues that you can help with in your school and/or community.

_____

_____

_____

_____

Now that you know some of the ways that you can play an active role in giving back, it is your responsibility to use these tools to make a difference. In order to achieve success in your life, you have to put others first and realize that there is a need in your community and a need in the world for someone like you to step up and lend a helping hand. Similar to what will be discussed in Chapter 12: Daniel Puder's Outlook on Bullying, you have to look beyond yourself and have compassion for others. A great place to start is by communicating with those around you about what your school and community is lacking and where there is a need. Once you have discovered where the need exists, you will be able to step up to the plate by getting your friends, family, and mentors involved in making your community a better place. You can always start by doing something small by yourself. But if you see a big need that requires a lot of help, I encourage you to get others involved to help you make a big difference.

Here is how you do it!

1. The best way to begin is to surround yourself with a great team or "think tank." This includes a group of your friends, family and mentors who can join together in order to come up with ideas and create plans to help complete the team mission.

Who do you want to be part of this?_____
_____
_____

2. Identify some areas of your community that could use some improvement.

What are they? _____
_____
_____

3. Do not hesitate to ask questions. Reach out to others in your community and ask questions of parents, teachers, police, firemen, and neighbors in order to find out some areas that could use some help.

Who will you ask? _____
_____
_____

4. State the issue and your goal(s) in this mission. _____
_____
_____

5. It's game plan time. Come up with a plan of how you can achieve your goal(s).

Short-term goal(s) _____
_____
_____
_____

Long-term goal(s) _____
_____
_____
_____

6. Creating a time line is crucial. Having a solid time line will help keep everyone involved on track with when the goal(s) will be met. Write down what that time line would include below.

_____
_____
_____
_____

7. Teamwork is crucial. Surround yourself with the right people to get the job done efficiently and effectively. Remember that you are only as strong as your weakest link. Everyone has different strengths and skills and it is important to recognize those strengths and skills in order to be able to achieve your goal with the right people in the right roles. This requires good interpersonal skills. Teams are always more successful than individuals when they are working together.

What strengths and or skills do you need to achieve your goal(s)? (Note taker, video maker, photographer, etc.). _____
_____
_____

Who are these people in your group? _____
_____
_____

8. Always think of the solution as being long-term. Most of the time, these types of outreach projects rely on consistency. The group involved in coordinating this project might want to make it ongoing (once a week, once a month, etc.) to ensure that your efforts are reaching their full potential in making a difference.

Now, I would like you to pledge that you will go out into your school and/or community and make a difference in the lives of others. Just start small and grow bigger with time. Always remember to keep your parents or guardian informed of what you are doing in the community and use the steps outlined above and do something that will make a difference. We need more people like you to make this world a better place!

Sign on the line to make a pledge to commit to taking part in something outside of yourself.

Name:_____Sign:_____ Date:_____

DP Quote: **"Civic responsibility takes thinking and acting outside of the box and shifting your focus from a 'me' mentality to a 'you' and 'we' mentality."**

"A true leader follows through, maintains a vision in the face of adversity, finds a way to turn problems into solutions, sees feedback as a gift, has the ability to empower a team, and lives to serve for the sake of the mission."

— Dr. David Puder, M.D., Division 1 National Rowing Champion

Chapter 11

THE SIX LEVELS OF LEADERSHIP

by David Puder, M.D.

Hi, my name is Dr. David Puder! My brother Daniel and I are very different people, but what we have in common is our motivation and commitment to help the next generation. I am a doctor who helps people get through some of their most difficult life situations. As a psychiatrist, I study the human dynamic and how people grow. I am interested in how things like what you eat, how you exercise, what you see, how you were raised, and how you choose to deal with your everyday issues contribute to your overall mental health. As a collegiate athlete who trained at a program that had the best coaches in the nation, I was able to experience a part of good leadership in action. As a medical student I co-led our class to adopt a hospital in Haiti (lluhaitiproject.org), and after the big earthquake, we were motivated to help thousands of people. I have also witnessed my father lead my family over the years, which I feel may be the most beautiful leadership I have ever seen.

Before we start, please answer these simple questions:

Do other people see you as a good leader? (Why or why not?)

_____

_____

How do you give or receive feedback, and what do you do with it?

_____

_____

When you run into a problem, what do you do?

_____

_____

How would you organize a team of people?

_____

_____

When you say you are going to do something, how often do you follow through?

_____

_____

Do you think a leader should be self-serving or a servant to his team?

_____

_____

Do you have a vision for where you are going?

_____

_____

You will see how these questions shape the content in this section. You can grow to become an amazing leader! No matter where you start from, you can do it! If right now, you feel that "No one would ever follow you," this material can help you radically transform your ability to successfully lead others.

If you follow the other chapters in this book carefully and really take them to heart, you will find yourself naturally a step ahead of most of the people around you, and therefore naturally fall into positions of leadership. I would like to provide six key foundational concepts used by life-changing leaders. As you find yourself in various leadership roles, you may want to reread these concepts over and over again until you master them.

Level One: Leaders Follow Through!

The first step to being a good leader is doing what you say you are going to do. This may seem very basic, but often I have seen leaders loose credibility with others by not following through with what they say they are going to do. The first thing is to only say you'll do what you know you can. In other words, don't make promises you know you can't keep! As a leader you set the tone for the group; if you are late, then everyone else will think it is OK to show up late. If you are not following through, how do you expect others to follow through?

Underline the ways below that may help you to follow through:

- Mark appointments or due dates for projects on a calendar

- Leave notes on your door or on your computer

- Set alarms on your phone

- Have your parent or guardian remind you

Write down some other methods that you can use to remember to follow through.

1. _____
2. _____
3. _____

Level Two: Leaders Put All Hardship into Perspective of the Vision or Goal!

Continually write down your goals. Know where you are going! When I trained for the national rowing championship, my goal was to win every race. It was so simple and so pure. Our coach would stand in front of us every morning and say, "Today we win the race! Today every stroke counts!" We continually saw our daily efforts as a small step toward our goal. Every painful moment had meaning. Every challenge put before us now would help us win later.

When I played football, many of the players slacked off at practice and saw it as worthless or boring. They would always say, "I am a game-day player." Then, when we would watch the game video, whenever they did not have the ball they ran half speed, and no one was fooled!

Sports are not the only area in which this occurs. In junior high or high school you may get away with not studying for a test, but as you go further and further in school, it will be hard to do well without a good work ethic. I was not the smartest freshman in high school, and I had to study all the time. When I got to college, I knew how to work hard and it paid off! My point is this: concentrate and give full attention to the small steps that will lead to the goal or vision you set out toward.

What are some small steps you will take today to move toward your goals?

1. _____
2. _____
3. _____

Level Three: Leaders Identify and Work Toward Solutions to Every Problem!

There may be obstacles in the way of achieving your goals. When you think you have failed, this needs to be seen not as a failure but as a problem in the process of achieving your goals. Level three leaders create growth out of various problems they encounter. They do not let problems stop them, They make adjustments to deal with the problem and become stronger leaders in the process. Rather than seeing failure as a dead end that stops you from moving forward, see the situation as an obstacle that you will have to overcome to keep moving towards your goals. For example, around December of my senior year at college at UC Berkeley, my rowing technique was still lacking. I was taken out of the main practices and told to row a one-person boat and re-learn how to row. My coach told me face to face, "David, you are a technical failure but still the strongest guy on the team." This was tough feedback, but true. I was extremely hard-working and one of the top three strongest guys on the team, but because my technique was not good, I made boats slower. Another one of my coaches saw me swelling up with tears and encouraged me by saying, "David, you can do it." I had a choice: either quit or overcome this obstacle. I remember rethinking how I would train. I had one last shot! At this point I was in this situation:

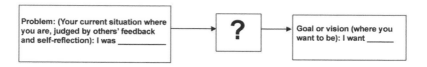

I could have become bitter and walked off the team, but I kept this in mind: feedback is information—feedback is a gift!

I was completely blind to my problem, and if my coach had been soft and not able to give me feedback I would have ended the season without accomplishing anything. Good leaders keep you moving toward the goal! Once you identify the problem, you can work to find a solution.

Four practical steps to create solutions to solve your problems:

1. *Ask for help. Find mentors and experts!* I found new coaches to meet with me one on one and I talked to the best athletes on my team about what they did to perfect their technique.
2. *Educate yourself. Read everything you can on the subject!* I read books on rowing techniques.
3. *Research. Watch videos of experts!* I found videos and watched them in slow motion to help me understand the motions.
4. *Practice. Work daily on building solutions!* I practiced 11 times per week.

After several months of practicing and improving my rowing technique, I was rowing completely differently, and my boat ended up winning the Pac-10 championship and went on to help our team win a team national championship! Now it's your turn: look at the goals that you wrote earlier and think about one problem you are having. You may need to get feedback from someone else before you can clearly describe your problem. Now go through the "four practical steps" and start to design your solution!

Fill in the boxes below.

Problem: → Solution: → Goal:

Level Four: Leaders See Feedback as a Gift!

What if your best friend was going to stop talking to you because you act/ like/do _____ (fill in the blank), but you had no idea it bothered him/her? What if you had three friendships in a row where you were continually making the same mistake? A lot of times, we are completely blind to how we are perceived or experienced by others. A level four leader will create a culture of openness where people will both learn from others how they can improve themselves and be able to give information in a genuine and nice way to others.

If you want to grow as a leader, you need to understand how others view you and then create a culture of openness. On a regular basis, ask how people are doing: "How is it to work on this project?" "How do you experience my leadership?" "Is there anything I could improve or learn?"

Creating a culture of openness can be very difficult! If you ask for feedback as a leader it will give others the opportunity to be heard. It will let others talk about some things that may bother them, and thus regardless of whether you believe it to be true, it can help diffuse the situation. Once they tell you something such as, "You are sometimes really bossy," take it as information, let them know you heard them, and tell them you will try to work on it. Often we have a completely different picture of ourselves than others do, so it's important to continue to have other people give us information about how they are experiencing us.

Believe it or not, I thought my technique was good before my coach made it really clear to me that it wasn't. I have learned (sometimes painfully) from past friends what I could improve on. A good leader is open to feedback, because they know it will help them grow!

How to give feedback:

- Ideally feedback should be asked for before you give it!

- Combine two good things you like about them with one constructive thing that could help them grow. For example: "I want to give you some feedback. I really like the energy you bring to this group. I think the group reacts negatively to you being chronically late. I really am grateful for your working hard on that project."

- Make sure it is understood by the person by asking, "What have you understood about what I just mentioned to you?" This should be given in a non-judgmental way.

- Make sure they can do something about it (i.e. don't tell someone their feet are too big, like girls used to tell me)

- Target the behavior not the person

- Try to give feedback right after you witnessed the behavior that you'd like to change

- Express the feeling you have when they do it (I feel sad when you...)

- Present the information as how you experience them and not as facts

- Give specific examples

You may have a hard time receiving feedback if you:

- Think you already know everything

- Think you have all the solutions

- Think you are perfect

- Have a lot of pride and are selfish

- Think that only others make mistakes

- Think any feedback is an attack against you personally

- Don't see feedback as a way to improve

How to receive feedback:

- Listen and give someone your full attention

- Don't defensive, don't look angry, and don't immediately deny their opinion of you

- Don't interrupt them. Listen and let them finish

- Allow them to know they were understood by repeating to them what

DANIEL PUDER

you heard (this may seem simple, but I have learned that people truly love being understood!)

• Take the feedback as information that you will process later (you may need to discuss it with your mentor)

• View it as a gift

• Realize that whether you agree or not, this is their opinion of you, which you can use improve yourself. After careful thought and evaluation, use the input if you think that it is helpful and beneficial to you.

Having lines of open feedback will save your relationships, future jobs, allow you to improve in all areas of your life, and inevitably change your life! When we give and receive feedback we continue to grow! Stay open and love it! Feedback is a gift!

Level Five: Leaders Empower Those on their Team!

When we were planning for the adoption of the hospital in Haiti, we had to clearly organize about twenty medical students into various jobs. We made an org (organizational) chart to help with this!

It is important to know what people are good at and what they enjoy. Learning how to hear their feedback will help you do this! You may even need to take other members of your team through this book or a similar program to find what they're passionate about. If people under your leadership have a passion for something, try to encourage them and give them support to get motivated. A level five leader positively changes the lives of those who serve on their team by empowering them while keeping things organized and on the right track toward the goal.

Doctor Hart is in charge of around twenty-six international hospitals around the world, and a level six leader. When I met with him to discuss adopting a hospital overseas, he saw our excitement and tried to help us accomplish what we wanted. He didn't want to put the brakes on our excitement, but rather to empower us to do what we wanted to do. Our methods were slightly different than his, but he was open to allowing us to thrive. His leadership causes positive changes in those he leads.

Different people's brains are "wired" to be good at different things and to enjoy different things. This world does not need another person who hates his job, but rather someone who is motivated to wake up and get to work! If you know things you are not as good at, like organizing, it is imperative to plan and place someone in that role. An org chart's purpose is to:

1. Show who is leading whom
2. Show who does what
3. Put people into their strengths

Here is the My Life My Power org chart:

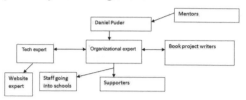

Notice how there is a flow of how things will be communicated (for example, the book writers work with the organizational expert, not with Daniel directly). This chart is very basic, and in reality maybe fifty people would be named as having different roles in My Life My Power. People are continually moved around to allow their skills to best be utilized. Part of empowerment is to positively change the lives of those you serve. If you are putting them in the places they will thrive, listening to their feedback, and empowering them to overcome their own roadblocks, you will be a leader who not only accomplishes great things but changes the lives of those around you!

In the space below, quickly create your own org chart for something you are a part of or desire to be a part of.

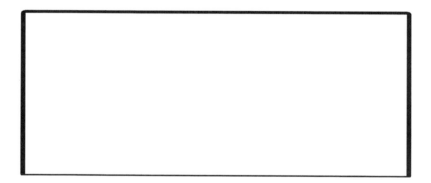

Level Six: Leaders Exhibit a Sacrificial Love!

Good leaders serve others and seek to lead out of a sacrificial love. I love the movie *Braveheart!* William Wallace risks his life to protect his wife from being raped; however, tragically, she ends up being murdered by those who had invaded his country. He goes on a quest to save the common people in his country from a similar fate. He fights endlessly for others, and people stand behind him. He went even to the point of death for what he believed in: the freedom of his people. His courage inspired thousands to finish his quest, and his country was liberated so that their wives would no longer be abused and they could live in freedom.

When I was in Haiti I witnessed Dr. Scott Nelson, an orthopedic surgeon, dedicate his time to take care of the "least of these." I was inspired and therefore rallied my class to adopt the hospital. His sacrificial leadership led me to help ignite a hundred future doctors to get behind a struggling hospital in Haiti. Our passion led to other classes doing likewise and now multiple hospitals have been adopted by medical school classes across the world. Sacrificial love creates movements.

When success comes and level six leaders are in the spotlight, because they see themselves as servant leaders, they turn the credit for their success back to those they serve. Rather then being prideful of their own accomplishments, they praise those that work under and around them. They let their team get the credit rather than themselves. Whenever they get a chance, they empower the team, rather then blowing their own horn.

This step is level six because you can't fake this level; you have to live it from your heart! You have to really believe that the team and the vision is more important then yourself.

This book also hopes to accomplish something powerful across the nation. Imagine our youth getting motivated. I have no idea how you will change the world, but imagine if we empowered each other to see that we can create positive change in the world!

Here are some steps to being a servant leader:

• Choose one long-term goal that will help others (this may start with building a strong family, for example)

• Make a point to build up those around you every day

• Decide that you will be teachable and continually receive feedback

• Serve your teammates by putting them into positions close to their gifting

• Empower those around you

• Make sacrifices to help those around you

• Give your team the credit for successes!

What would need to occur for you to become a leader? _____
_____
_____

PART TWO:
MY POWER

"Learning how to achieve success in all aspects of my life has been a very important tool for me becoming successful as a young actor. My Life My Power's program will teach you how to achieve your full potential while having fun and enjoying life. These concepts and tips are so important and will stay with me for my entire life's journey! Dream big!"

— Kenton Duty, Actor, Musician, Disney Channel series *Shake It Up,* and ABC series, *Lost*

CHAPTER 12:

DANIEL PUDER'S OUTLOOK ON BULLYING

by Daniel Puder, Brittney Lozano

I know everyone looks at me now as Daniel Puder, the big, blond, unde-feated MMA fighter and pro wrestler. However, when I was a kid, I was in special education and was one of the slowest kids in the mile run in the sixth grade. I was teased, bullied, and picked on.

When I was in elementary school, my brother David (who is two years younger than me) and I were being picked on and bullied by a group of kids. There were times when people would call me dumb and stupid because I went to a "special room" for classes to help me learn in different ways. Other times, people would tease me and make fun of me because I wasn't very good at sports.

We continued to be bullied until we finally decided to tell our dad about what was going on. The very next day, he went to our school to talk to the teachers and administration, who put an immediate stop to the bullying. Looking back, the crazy part was that my brother and I were good kids. We minded our own business and we both worked hard in school. However, because I was seen as "different" for my learning disability, I became an easy target for bullying, and since my brother was always with me, he became a target as well.

So, next time you see a kid who is handicapped, disabled, in special educa-tion, or just different than you, I encourage you to put your hand out, look them in the eye, and tell them you will be their friend. By doing this, other people will respect you for being a team player and for showing compassion toward others. If you find that your peers start to tease you or bully you for helping someone else, remember that those people are actually strug-gling with something much deeper that you can't always see on the surface. There is something going on in their lives that makes them feel the need to criticize others in order to make themselves feel better. In the long run, it is good to have friends and friendlies, not enemies. I urge you to take time to help others and to leave a positive, lasting impression those around you who might be different from you.

As you read through this chapter, remember to keep an open mind and be conscious of how others feel about this serious topic of bullying.

Circle how often you either experience or witness bullying.

a. Daily (if so, how many times a day?) _____
b. Weekly
c. Monthly

Circle where you notice that the bullying typically occurs.

a. At school
b. On the way to or from school
c. At home
d. Online
e. Other (if so, where?) _____

Answer the following questions honestly about how you view bullying. Circle the number that best fits how you feel about each question depending on how strongly you agree or how strongly you disagree. Use the chart below for reference.

Strongly Agree	Agree	Somewhat Agree	Somewhat Disagree	Disagree	Strongly Disagree
1	2	3	4	5	6

1. When I see someone being bullied, I feel sad.
     1   2   3   4   5   6
2. Everyone deserves to feel safe and secure in school.
     1   2   3   4   5   6
3. When I hear a rumor about someone, I pass it along.
     1   2   3   4   5   6
4. He/she is being bullied because they deserve it.
     1   2   3   4   5   6
5. I want to help the bullied victim, but don't know how to.
     1   2   3   4   5   6
6. The bully needs to pick on someone his/her own size.
     1   2   3   4   5   6
7. My school does a good job of controlling bullying.
     1   2   3   4   5   6
8. I am not embarrassed to stand up for others.
     1   2   3   4   5   6

9. The person being bullied needs to toughen up.

     1   2   3   4   5   6

10. Bullies only do it to make themselves feel better.

     1   2   3   4   5   6

There are four main types of bullying. Below we discuss what the different types of bullying are. After you read about each type of bullying, I want you to write down some of the thoughts that first come to your mind about that particular type of bullying.

PHYSICAL

Physical bullying is the most noticeable type of bullying, as it includes physical violence toward another person. This type of bullying involves any form of physical contact in which the bully uses their strength to overpower the victim through physical actions.

What are your thoughts? Have you ever seen this? _____

_____

_____

_____

_____

VERBAL

Verbal bullying can cause just as much harm as physical bullying. It occurs when the victim is being threatened, insulted, or talked to in an abusive or hurtful way. When someone verbally abuses another person, the intent is to belittle and degrade the victim. With verbal bullying, it is important to remember that words have powerful effects and can cause just as much damage as physical bullying.

What are your thoughts? Have you ever seen this? _____

_____

_____

_____

_____

SOCIAL

Social bullying occurs when someone is treated by others as an outsider and socially isolated. This can involve the spreading of rumors, excluding someone from activities and events, deliberately ignoring the person, and tearing down someone's social status. All of these things can have serious emotional effects which can unfortunately stay with that person for their entire life.

What are your thoughts? Have you ever seen this? _____

_____
_____
_____
_____

CYBER

Cyber bullying has been on the rise due to the number of youth using technology. With this type of bullying, the victim is terrorized through text messaging, emails, chat rooms, blogging, social networking, instant messaging, etc. Because things that are put on the Internet are accessible to anyone, the damage that this type of bullying causes is huge!

What are your thoughts? Have you ever seen this? _____

_____
_____
_____
_____

Have you ever been bullied? If so, circle which type(s) of bullying you experienced.

Physical   Verbal   Social   Cyber

Other_____

Have you ever been a bully? If so, circle which type(s) of bullying you may have done.

Physical   Verbal   Social   Cyber

Other_____

Can you think of any other type of bullying that you have either seen, done, or experienced? If so, what type of actions were involved?

_____
_____
_____

Now that we know what some of the different types of bullying are, and what they involve, let's talk about some of the effects that bullying can have. You might think that bullying only affects one person: the person being bullied. However, the truth is that bullying also affects those that witness the bullying and the bully themselves. Here's how:

For the person being bullied: Bullying can cause the victim to develop stress and anxiety from the fear of being bullied, which, in turn, distracts them from being able to focus or being able to engage in the classroom. It can cause them to feel powerless, weak, lonely, depressed, to develop low self-esteem, experience physical sickness, and can increase their tendencies to socially isolate themselves, which leads them to feeling even more alone. As humans, we often identify with how others perceive us; therefore, the victim of bullying can sometimes begin to believe that the names he/she is being called are accurate—even when they are not. This, in turn, causes even more depression and, in extreme cases, can lead to suicide. Believe it or not, even after graduating from high school, the person being bullied can continue to experience long-term effects, such as a continued depression and low self-esteem.

If you have ever been bullied, can you relate to these feelings described above? Yes   No

Are there any feelings that you have experienced that were not described above? If so, what are they?

_____

_____

_____

_____

_____

For the bully: Yes, even the bully can experience negative effects from their actions. Bullying is often a learned behavior and may indicate that the bully was either bullied themselves at one time or another, or that there is something else going on in their lives that is reflected in how they treat others. Usually the person bullies other people to feel better about themselves, to feel powerful, or to get attention from others. Someone who is a bully often becomes involved in other serious negative behaviors. Some of these behaviors include dropping out of school, drug and alcohol abuse, stealing, and fighting.

If you have ever been a bully, can you relate to the things described above? Yes   No

Are there any feelings or reasons for being a bully that were not described above? If so, what are they?

_____

_____

_____

_____

_____

For the witness of bullying: I think it would be safe to say that we have all witnessed bullying at one time or another in our lives. Bullying can affect the witness by causing them to feel helpless, anxious, or stressed. It can cause the witness to feel the need to end a friendship or to avoid being seen with the person being bullied because it could lead to them being bullied as well. It can also cause the witness to feel guilty for not stepping in or standing up for the person being bullied. For some witnesses, the feeling of guilt might be rationalized in your own mind by the idea that the victim deserved to be bullied, but the truth is NO ONE deserves to be put down and abused by someone else. So it is important to always help others who are in need.

If you have witnessed bullying, can you relate to the feelings described above? Yes   No

Are there any feelings that you've experienced that were not described above? If so, what are they?

_____

_____

_____

_____

_____

Think back on a time when you were bullied or witnessed bullying happen. Write down some words of how it made you feel directly after. Then circle a number to represent how strong that particular feeling was for you (1 being not very strong, 5 being very strong). Examples might include feeling helpless, angry, lonely, sad, scared, etc.

	Not Very Strong	-	Neutral	-	Very Strong
_____	1	2	3	4	5
_____	1	2	3	4	5
_____	1	2	3	4	5
_____	1	2	3	4	5

For those of you who have been bullied or are currently being bullied, below are some helpful tips to overcome a bully's attacks.

Walk away: Easier said than done, right? Trust me, I know from personal experience that this is not always an easy task. It will be tough to ignore their insults, but take it from first-hand experience, eventually the bully will get bored with you because you will be showing them that you don't care. Even if it is eating you up on the inside to hear their hurtful words, it would be better to save face for the time being and then talk to someone that you trust about it afterward, rather than fueling the bully's fire by showing them how much it affects you. Remember that one of the main reasons that people choose to bully a particular person is because they think that they are vulnerable to attacks. If you are able to hold your head high and show them that you will not give in to their insults, they will move on and leave you alone. But it is important to remember that after you have walked away, you need to talk to someone about it so that you don't keep all your feelings and emotions bottled up.

It's NOT always best to fight back: Just like walking away from the bully when they are verbally abusing you, similar advice goes for when a bully tries to physically abuse you through fighting. While the bully is wrong in their actions, you have to keep in mind that participating in the fight puts you at risk for either getting hurt or getting in trouble. For instance, I remember one day when I was in school and I was being pushed around by a bully. Something inside of me told me to fight back, and so I did, only to find myself in the principal's office. I almost got suspended from school. Even though the bully was the one who instigated the fight, I was still a participant in it and therefore I got in trouble as well. I urge you to not to give in to your inner voice, which may tell you to fight back physically. This may create a bigger problem for you in the end.

Don't handle it on your own: It is important to always remember that you are not alone and that it is okay to involve an adult. Don't ever think that you are any less of a person because you have to get someone older to help put an end to the bullying you are experiencing. Within your school, there are numerous resources available to you that offer the support and assistance that you need. Guidance counselors, school police officers, teachers, parents, and any other adult who is in charge has the ability to get the necessary people involved on your behalf. If you are worried that the bully might find out you told someone about the situation, you can always make it very clear to the person you are telling that you want to keep the information anonymous. Also, know that the person that you go to for help will not judge you and that they will believe you. If for some reason they don't take action against the situation for you, don't be discouraged, just find someone else to tell until the problem stops. But truly, the adults are there to help and make sure that you are not only safe, but that you feel safe as well.

It's time for friends: Having someone to talk to can make a huge impact. One thing that a bully looks for when finding someone to pick on is someone who is all alone. Even if you feel like you don't have any friends, just surrounding yourself with other people and not being in an empty area can keep you from being in a situation that may cause you to be more vulnerable and allow the bullying to take place. Being able to talk to a friend can greatly help the way that you feel about yourself and also be a way for you to talk through your feelings. Friends can help uplift you when you are feeling depressed, and being able to have a support system of people who are on your side will go a long way.

Know that you deserve success: This is probably the most important piece of advice that I can give you when it comes to the steps you can take to overcome a bully. When you are getting picked on, just know that, as I mentioned earlier, it's NOT you. I can't even begin to count all of the times that I was bullied growing up. Even when I became an adult and started fighting professionally in both the WWE and MMA, people felt the need to negatively critique me and found ways to put me down. Throughout everything, I had to remember to tell myself that I do deserve happiness and success. As challenging as it can be to keep your head up and overcome their bullying, in the end, you will be the bigger person and you will be the one to achieve the ultimate prize of success. The character qualities that you will have gained from learning how to hold your head high, stay confident, and know that you deserve the best will get you farther in life that you could ever imagine.

Daniel Puder's Personal Story

Now, let me tell you about someone I met personally in Los Angeles who gave me insight into bullying. I was training a few fighters at my gym in Hollywood, CA, when a kid came up to me and said, "Hey Daniel, can I talk to you? I yelled at my best friend today." I stopped what I was doing and sat down with him to listen to what was going on in his life. I asked him if he had apologized to his friend and he said that he had. I asked, "How is life at school and home treating you?" He replied, "Everything is great." At this point, I started to think to myself that everything couldn't be great if he was lashing out at one of his best friends. So, I continued to ask him other questions about his life and in his response, he replied, "Well, my therapist..." and I thought to myself, well, if a thirteen-year-old kid has a therapist, then something is going on in his life. I then asked him how long he'd had a therapist for and he went on to tell me he had been seeing his therapist for two years. I asked him what had happened a couple of years ago in his life that he needed to see a therapist, and he ended up telling me that his father had a heart attack and couldn't box with him anymore, his mother lost her baby the day after he got into a fight with her, and his grandmother and grandfather died-all within a year.

The thing that stunned me was, here was an amazing kid who was being shaped by instances around him that he had absolutely no control over. The things that were going on in his life were completely out of his hands, and yet they were affecting him and his relationships with others. When he yelled at his friend, it wasn't because he was a bad person, or because he wanted to hurt his friend's feelings. It had a lot to do with the fact that he had so many other things going on in his life and he was trying to figure out how to cope with all of those feelings. But without having some solid direction, he was unaware of how to properly channel his hurt.

What this young boy taught me is that often people who lash out at others have something much bigger going on in their own lives to cause such hurt and pain. So, when you see something like this happening, where someone is lashing out at other people for what seems like no reason at all, take a moment to ask them some simple questions, like, "How is your day going?" "Is everything okay at home?" "How are you doing in school?" Truly, just showing them that you care will make a huge difference in their perspective on life—just remember to always be a good friend and make sure your friends know you care about them.

Have you ever treated someone poorly because of something that you might be personally dealing with? If so, what happened and how did you get through that situation?

_____
_____
_____

Daniel Puder's Closing Thoughts on Bullying

If you are being bullied, I want you to know that you are NOT alone. Remember how earlier in the chapter, I was telling you about my personal experience with bullying? Well, that is something that was almost an everyday occurrence for me. I couldn't understand why these bullies felt the need to be so mean to me and what I did to deserve it. But the truth is, I hadn't done anything to deserve their bullying. It wasn't me that had a problem, it was them. As soon as I allowed myself to realize that I deserved more than their cruel words and physical abuse, I was able to pull myself out of the depression and loneliness that I felt.

If you are a bully, I want you to know that this does not mean that you are a bad person. You are AMAZING! We all know what it feels like to be angry, frustrated, confused, bored, or stressed out. You might feel like bullying someone helps to relieve those feelings. But I am telling you right now that when you wake up the next morning, those feelings will still be there waiting for you. Hurting someone else only serves to take you one step further from becoming successful in your own life. You may have learned how to be a bully from personal experience in your own household, from the things that you watch on television, or from the music that you listen to. Regardless of the reason or where you may have picked up on those habits, it is important to know that there is no excuse. You've taken a huge step in taking the time to read through this book, and I guarantee that if you are able to put into practice the information and tools I have provided you with, you have the ability to become so successful in your life that you will have neither the desire nor the time to be a bully. Just know that it is never too late to change and take a stand for your future. You deserve it!

No matter what role you may play in bullying—the person being bullied, the bully, or the person witnessing the bullying—I want you to remember one thing: we are not all that different from one another. Let's go back to one of the questions that I asked you at the beginning of this chapter, which was, "Do you want to be successful in life?" I can almost guarantee you that if everyone answered that question honestly, there would be a unanimous answer of "YES!" This is one thing that you already know you have in common with your peers. My goal is to make sure that all of you know that the information you have been provided in this book will lead you in the right direction toward success. At the end of the day, we are not all that different from one another and we all want to be successful and make something of ourselves. If we can each learn how to be kind to others, focus on our own accomplishments, and build up our own positive character qualities, then we really do have the ability to make a difference, not only in our school and our community, but in our own lives as well.

Sign on the line to make a pledge to treat everyone with respect and to take a stand against bullying. This pledge says that if you are being bullied, you will always remember that you are NOT the problem, that you are an amazing person, and that you deserve happiness. If you are the person bullying others, you are pledging to stop and to be kind to others because no matter what is going on in your life, nobody deserves to feel pain and hurt. And if you are witnessing bullying happen, you are pledging to stand up for others and to be a friend to someone who needs encouragement.

Name:_____Sign:_____Date:_____

DANIEL PUDER

Here are a few things to do if you or someone you know needs help with bullying:

Write down what the situation is and make two copies so that you have written documentation. Sign both copies and make sure that the person you report the situation to signs both copies as well so that you have written proof that they received it. Keep one copy for yourself in a safe place and leave one copy with the person to whom you reported the situation. Remember to follow up with the person you report the situation to.

1. Talk to your parents or guardian

2. Go to a teacher, principal, or school counselor and tell them what is going on

3. If you think what happened may have been a crime, go to your local police station and make a report

4. Visit www.MyLifeMyPower.org and look in the "Causes" section for useful information and resources

"Never underestimate the power of hard work and determination. Working hard in school and keeping a positive outlook on life will ensure success and happiness. The My Life My Power program teaches that the power to overcome any obstacle is within you!"

—Mike O'Hearn, "Titan" from the hit TV show *American Gladiators*, four-time Mr. Universe, Strongman Champion, Judo Champion.

Chapter 13

EXERCISE FOR LIFE!

by David Puder, M.D.

I would love to impart a few words of wisdom on the basics of how to be an excellent athlete by sharing things I have learned at different phases of my life. I want to be able to help you make exercising something that you enjoy and succeed at and to teach you valuable lessons about life. I also want to open up your mind to how exercise might empower you to reach new academic levels, help you concentrate more in school, and succeed at your goals even if they are not directly related to exercise at all!

I was not always athletic; in fact, I was one of the most obese and slowest kids in elementary school. In fourth grade I was so overweight that kids made fun of me on a regular basis. My mom noticed something was wrong and pulled me out of public school and put me in a small private school. I remember being happy, as kids were nice to me and wanted to be my friend...but I was still 185 pounds in fifth grade! During fifth and sixth grade I basically did no athletic activity. I preferred art, reading and music.

By seventh grade, however, my interest in sports began to change. I played flag football and began to ride the bike my father got for me. My football coach, an ex-Marine, demonstrated tough love by making me run throughout what seemed to be the entirety of every practice. A funny thing happened: I began to enjoy working out as my body composition changed from mostly fat to mostly muscle. Following football, I played basketball and, after I did not make the soccer team (I was still clumsy), I began working out at a gym. By asking people questions and reading books and magazines, I taught myself how to lift weights and learned general concepts of physical health.

The main fitness principles I learned from that period of my life:

• Change up your workout at least every month. You can really get stuck doing the same types of workout every week, but if you change your exercise routine regularly, you will see the greatest growth in your athletic ability. The body needs to be shocked and stressed in new ways to make the largest gains. This truth was reinforced continually as I moved on in sports.

• Use big muscle groups. Engage in activities where all your muscles are being activated at once rather than doing simple isolated movements. Examples include swimming, running, rowing, squat jumps, lunges, pushups, pull-ups, etc.

- Diet and sleep play a role in maximizing your performance. (You can read about this in the lifestyle chapter of this book.)

- Find mentors, read books and watch videos to perfect the proper technique for various exercises. Be a true student of whatever you put your mind to!

Out of the key fitness principles, what are some detailed things you could do differently?

Ways to vary your workout _____

Ways to use big muscle groups_____

Who could help you learn? _____

What is the next step to finding a book or video on the technique of your sport? _____

By the time I reached high school, I was 6 feet, 5 inches tall, but still weighed 185 pounds. I continued to play football and my brother persuaded me to give wrestling a try. In the first year of wrestling, I felt like vomiting before every practice in fear of the pain I was about to go through. I'd feel the same way after practice for what I had just experienced. I worked out harder than I had ever done in my life, and found I had a love/hate relationship with the sport. After several years of wrestling, I went from losing most of my matches to winning most of my matches, and even winning some tournaments. I also became a football team captain, and led our offense as a tight-end. During that phase of my life, I learned how to push through my pain, and go further than I thought was possible. I learned how to contribute to a team. I learned that I could work out twice a day and my body would recover and be stronger if I had proper rest and nutrition.

Here are some practical tips that you can apply to any sport:

- Challenge yourself daily and push your limits

- Make a workout schedule and train in a way that will help you obtain your goals

- Do some light cardio (like jogging) for twenty to forty minutes before school. This will help you concentrate in your classes and help build your aerobic base.

- Be teachable and approach every practice with the thought that you are going to utilize the time to get in shape and become more technical.

- Find activities that develop cardiovascular endurance. One way might be to break a basketball game into three-on-three, a soccer or football game into four-on-four. Smaller teams will get you running around more and give you more time to work on the basics of sport.

• Learn and use the proper technique, then repeat it over and over so that it becomes muscle memory. When you have good technique programmed into you, you won't have to think so hard about what you are doing; it becomes automatic, especially under pressure. They say that it takes 10,000 hours of doing something to be world-class—so keep practicing!

Due to my success in wrestling and football, I was recruited to row at Cal Berkeley by Geoff Bond. Rowing involves four to eight people in a boat moving in tandem on slides in a motion that uses all of your major muscle groups at the same time (legs, glutes, abs, back, shoulders, arms). Rowing is like running up a hill with a neck collar connected to seven other guys. If one person slows down then everyone is choked to death. Due to the competitive environment of the team, our collective physical endurance was taken to the next level. For example, as a team we ran up Half Dome my freshmen year, something I don't think I would ever do alone or for fun! My motivation to row and work hard was enhanced by my love for the people on my team. I think a large portion of my success was due to learning how to remain humble and teachable. A student group called Athletes in Action allowed me to learn how to see rowing as a gift and remain humble. There is a balance between having confidence and knowing that you don't know everything and can still make improvements. Learning how to be a good team member and receive feedback and collectively overcome problems has taught me lessons that have transferred over into other areas of my life.

Here is a summary of things I learned during college about how to perform at a high level:

• There is joy in becoming fully invested in a team, building faith and trust in one another, and working hard toward a common goal

• Set a long term athletic goal as a team and then keep that in mind during your daily efforts

• Learn how to set a schedule in both your individual and collective practices and then actually do what you planned to do. This builds discipline. For example, if you go into a workout saying you are going to run for thirty minutes, and then at twenty minutes feel like walking, choose instead to complete what you set out to do and push through!

• Sometimes it is harder to work out alone, but it allows you to become stronger mentally and physically

• Realize that you can go harder and longer than you think possible

- Learn how to concentrate on the task at hand. Don't worry about past mistakes (which were part of your growth) or future failures (you should have hope for the future), but rather concentrate on your current task. For example, in rowing I would try to concentrate on the current stroke, and not think or worry about anything else.

During my four years of medical school and my current work as a doctor, I did and do sports mainly for enjoyment, but also find that it optimizes my ability to study and learn. I love going for an early morning run and catching the beauty of a sunset. I try to run outside because I enjoy nature, and choose dirt paths if possible as they are kinder on my knees. I have found that running in the mountains is the most enjoyable, as running up hills is an amazing workout, but you may enjoy different things. I love my road bike, and once rode from Canada to California with a tent on my trailer. I have also taught myself to swim, mainly by reading a book on swimming and watching slow-motion videos on the Internet of expert swimmers in action. I lift weights, during which I do super-sets, which build muscular endurance. For example, I do bench, the rowing machine, pull-downs, three different shoulder movements, and squats, all moving quickly from machine to machine without rest. I love to go on day hikes up in the mountains. I am preparing to eventually do some triathlons, but mainly do sports for enjoyment and the mental and physical benefits I gain from them!

Do you ever wonder why doing sports makes people healthier, happy, smarter and more confident? From my coursework in molecular cell biology at Berkeley Medical School and my continued curiosity, I have learned why exercise is so powerful! Exercise is like Miracle-Gro for the brain. In the same way alcohol or drugs can damage your brain, exercise can help your brain grow! With good intensity exercise, your brain naturally produces BDNF (brain-derived neurotrophic factor), which causes your brain to sprout new connections and grow. When your body is then stressed by practicing new movements, new pathways are produced in the brain that better enable the body to do the same movements in the future. Combining exercise-producing BDNF (Miracle-Gro) with an environment of learning causes you to perform at a much higher level. In one study, kids who ran for approximately thirty minutes prior to classes absorbed 62% more material than kids who did not exercise. Some schools with strong physical education programs have been shown to score higher on standardized tests!

Here is a brief summary of the effects of exercise on the brain. Some of this may be a bit scientific, but perhaps you can look into these things more after you have some good exercise.

- Endurance types of exercise increase BDNF, which stimulates new connections between nerves and increases the capacity for the brain to change

- The area of your brain that coordinates the storing of new data (the hippocampus) increases in both number of cells and connections. So memorizing things (like vocabulary) will be optimized after a good workout!

- Exercise improves frontal lobe function. This is the area of the brain that makes decisions and sets goals, thinks of creative solutions to problems, enables you to concentrate, and is even part of your ability to have compassion for others. Lack of sleep as well as alcohol and other addictions tend to reduce the function of the frontal lobe, whereas after a good workout, the function of this part of your brain will be increased.

- Exercise modulates, and thus optimizes, your neurotransmitters (serotonin, norepinephrine, dopamine). Some studies show that a daily session of exercise is as good as one antidepressant or one anti-anxiety medication! The antidepressant effect may take several weeks, but people tend to feel less anxious during and directly after even one good workout. As a doctor, I sometimes see people who are severely depressed and even suicidal. I always tell them that exercise will be part of their transformation into peak mental health.

- When you practice something like catching a ball, at first you have to bring high levels of concentration (frontal lobe) to your activity. Eventually it becomes second nature after new pathways are created and the pathways of your brain get stronger (by laying down myelin). When you come to game day, the strenuous exercise will cause your frontal lobe not to work as well because your blood is going to your muscles; therefore, you will need to have strong pathways set up. So, before having a technical workout, get ten to fifteen minutes of exercise that gets your heart rate up!

For a better understanding of how exercise enhances your brain, and more explanation of the above material, read *Spark: The Revolutionary New Science of Exercise and the Brain* by Dr. John J. Ratey.

Some other general thoughts on things I have learned: _____
_____
_____
_____
_____

Optimizing your power center!

Most athletic movement comes from the hips. If you squat down and jump up with all your force, that is the same movement used in all athletic events to some degree. For example, in baseball, batters explode through the hips to hit the ball. In swimming, you connect your hips with your arms in your kick. In running, hips provide the explosion that gets you going and up hills. In football, hips explode you from the line and accelerate you into your opponent. In basketball, your hips provide most of the force acting on the ball as you make your shot. In tennis the movement of your hips brings the power to the ball. Often people lift weights for their upper body only; however, this is a huge mistake because most of the athletic movement is controlled by your hips and utilizes your legs. Your abdominal muscles connect your hips to your upper body. So it's imperative to strengthen them to prevent injuries and utilize the full strength of your legs.

Here are some basic thoughts on increasing hip strength:

• Do jump squats (slowly go down and then explode up). Add some weights but keep your jumps explosive!

• Learn how to do squats and lunges with the correct technique (start light with high reps and correct technique)

• Find a steep hill and do sprints up it in sets of 5-10. (By creating leg strength through weighted squats and lunges and also explosive strength by jumping and hill sprints, you will quickly have a huge advantage in any sport that requires strong hips).

On monitoring your heart rate:

I highly recommend investing $30 in a heart-rate monitor. This can act as a way to monitor your effort. If you journal to track your workouts, you can add in your average heart rate and data from the watch. I think coaches and PE teachers would benefit from monitoring effort as measured by their athletes' heart rate. For example, someone who is out of shape may run an eleven-minute mile with a heart rate that is 90% of their maximum and thus should be congratulated.

You can calculate your maximum heart rate by subtracting your age from 220. For example: 220 - 20 (years old) = 200. What is your maximum heart rate (MHR)?_____

Then find your heart rate zones by multiplying your MHR by 0.5, 0.6, 0.7, 0.8, and 0.9, and write them in the spaces below:

Zone 5: VO2 Max (max effort): 90%-100% _____

Zone 4: Anaerobic (hard core): 80-90% _____

Zone 3: Aerobic (endurance): 70-80% _____

DANIEL PUDER

Zone 2: Fitness (fat burn): 60-70% _____

Zone 1: Fitness (fat burn): 50-60%_____

"Being healthy is about caring for your body so that you will live a long and happy life. Feeling good and looking good are extra perks. Healthy choices make happy people."

— Carolyn Quijano, MS, RD

DANIEL PUDER

Chapter 14

FOOD FOR LIFE

by David Puder, M.D., Co-Author Carolyn Quijano

Why have a chapter on nutrition in this book? Well, food plays a bigger role in our lives than you may think. Food affects your health, your weight, the way you feel, and how you think. Simply put, we really are, in part, what we eat. This chapter is necessary because over 66% of Americans are overweight, and the number one cause of death in America is heart disease. These two facts are not a coincidence. Eating right can optimize your overall well-being. Being healthy doesn't just make you thin, it enhances your body's ability to perform physically and mentally. This chapter will discuss how food will help you succeed.

Before we start, let's recall what you ate yesterday. Don't be afraid to write down everything, including all beverages and snacks.

Breakfast:

_____

_____

Drinks/Snacks:

_____

_____

Lunch:

_____

_____

Drinks/Snacks:

_____

_____

Dinner:

_____

_____

Drinks/Snacks:

_____

_____

When I (David) was in fifth grade, I weighed 185 pounds. I needed help! I ate so much candy and fast food that my weight became out of control. I became interested in health in junior high when I began lifting weights and playing basketball and flag football. I started asking people at the gym how to get buff. I read tons of health magazines and books. These books contained various opinions and ideas on dieting and health that were sometimes contradictory. I saw a common theme that various diets or programs would transform you into the "perfect body" in 10-30 days. I started taking supplements and participated in various workout programs that required me to work out every day. I look back and realize that I was missing the big picture.

In high school, I wanted to improve my health so that I could be an exceptional athlete. I was on the wrestling team, and I had to cut weight fast! I remember losing twenty pounds in two months. (This was not healthy!) While in college I was working out three to five hours per day. I had to eat enough food to fuel my body for a quick recovery. At that point, I realized eating more whole grains, fruits, and veggies improved my recovery time and studying capabilities. I slowly made changes to how I approached food. First, I started eating more and more fruits and veggies. I taught myself how to cook (and I am still learning.) Next, I cut out all soda and tried to stick to mainly drinking water. I slowly stopped eating anything that could be called "junk food," meaning I was not eating fast food or anything super processed. This is when I started to understand the term of eating "whole foods."

In medical school I learned foundational material about nutrition, but my curiosity kept me reading deeper and deeper. Randomly I stumbled upon a few books on nutrition that changed my outlook and helped my brain perform at a high level. I found that if I ate certain foods I could study without getting a "food coma." This was important because I was studying from eight in the morning to ten at night. I started reading scientific journal articles, which are what reliable science-based books use as references! This is when my eyes were really opened to the power of a good diet. I quickly realized that all those "health" magazines I had relied on in the past were a distorted version of the truth, often telling people what they want to hear. Now when I glance at magazines on health, I think to myself, I wish I could tell others the truth about food.

Carolyn, a dietitian, and I have outlined basic concepts to guide you to a lifetime of optimal health. To become a dietitian, Carolyn studied nutrition for four years in college, and continued on to get her Masters in nutrition. Eating healthy is not just about being thin or physically fit. It's about taking care of yourself! And when you take care of yourself, you will naturally be your ideal body weight. We will discuss what you shouldn't do (fad diets), what you should do (eat whole foods), and how to do it (rearrange your plate). It is our hope that you take this information as encouragement to change your eating behaviors and achieve a happy and healthy life.

Food for Life #1: Stop dieting!

Regardless of what the latest magazine or infomercial says, there are no secrets or magical fixes to being healthy. So honestly, stop dieting. Dieting is a deceptive short-term solution. Diets are not made to be long term. So once you stop dieting, all those unhealthy habits you were trying to stop come back! Dieting can take you on an emotional roller coaster of happiness, guilt, and disappointment. Dieting plays tricks on your brain. Dieting can make you feel restricted and trapped and may encourage using food as a reward. "I've been good this week, so I can have a piece of cake" should never be a thought that enters your mind. Dogs get food rewards, not people. While you should enjoy the food you eat, food should never be a means of happiness. Dieting will ultimately create negative self-talk and make you feel bad if you don't succeed. You are accepted and valued not from your performance, but for who you are now.

Food should not bring you feelings of worry or anxiety either. Good, healthy food should be seen as a blessing. Instead of going crazy on some restrictive fad diet, think about being someone who has decided to eat healthy food. Identify yourself as a healthy individual who would rather eat healthy because you value yourself. See what you eat as a way of life rather then something you do for a number of days. You can do it!

Food For Life #2: Eat whole foods!

So if you aren't dieting, what are you doing? Eating whole foods. Whole foods are anything that can be classified as a plant: vegetables, fruits, whole grains, nuts, and beans. Well, French fries are a potato, right? Yes, but they have been skinned (removing the fiber) and deep fried (adding a bunch of saturated fat). So it's not only eating plant foods, but it's also staying away from processed food. This means you should try to avoid food that comes in a package, was made in a factory, or has been deep fried.

We recommend that when people go shopping, they begin in the produce section, which is where we spend the majority of our time. We are looking for the unprocessed foods, the foods that will go bad if you don't eat them in a week or so. After the produce section, we go to the dried food aisle. There we pick up a few things like kidney beans, black beans, pinto beans, lentils, split peas, brown rice, barley, or oats. We may go to the canned food section where we can buy canned beans, tomato sauces, coconut milk, or olives. Bread is considered a processed food, but as long as you are getting a whole grain bread, you're good to go. Nuts, while a little pricey, are a great source of fat and protein. We buy a variety of nuts at grocery stores that sell them in bins. This way, we get a better deal, and it's worth it! Nuts are high in healthy fats and can reduce your risk for heart disease. Our last stop in the grocery store is the frozen section. Here, we may pick up a couple bags of frozen veggies, like peas, corn, or string beans.

If cooking isn't your thing, you can find prepackaged, microwavable brown rice packets, edamame (soybeans), and lentil dishes. Just remember to look at the label to make sure you know what you're eating. Packaged foods are sneaky! You never know what's been done to the food, and just because the package looks healthy doesn't mean that it is.

These prepackaged convenience foods can be expensive, so it's good to learn how to prepare your own dishes. Buying a lot of fresh produce may be unrealistic for you at the moment. Don't worry, frozen veggies are just as nutritious as fresh. We prefer the taste of fresh vegetables, but frozen vegetables may be an easier transition to beginning a new healthy lifestyle. Frozen berries are often cheaper than fresh berries and just as delicious.

Remember, start where you feel most comfortable. Small changes can make a huge difference. Buy a bag of baby carrots instead of a bag of chips, try a whole grain cereal instead of a sugary one, or buy whole wheat bread instead of white. One big change I made was from drinking soda to drinking water. Try having a fruit for a dessert instead of cookies or ice cream.

Earlier in the chapter, David had mentioned his being overweight due to consistently eating fast food and not knowing how to cook! But, he made a decision to get healthy one step at a time. Now he buys his produce at farmers markets, he only buys freshly made whole grain bread, and he even has his own garden! Although David is a pretty healthy person, he continues to find new ways to enjoy delicious meals that are also super healthy!

Food for Life #3: Rearrange your plate! Literally!

The ideal diet has four sections: grains, vegetables, fruit, and protein. Let's explore these together.

Grains: The complex source of carbohydrates

Consider that the human body is like a car, where the brain and muscles would be considered the engine, and filling your stomach with food is like filling your car with gas. In a car, the gas provides energy for it to run. In the same way, the food you eat provides energy for your daily activities.

Carbohydrates are our main fuel source. Despite what you've heard, carbs are good for you—the key is getting the right carbs. Simple carbs, found in soda, white bread, and ice cream, are easily absorbed in your body and are quickly used as energy or stored as fat. This would be like giving your car gas that makes it go so fast that it hits other cars and has no fuel left to get to where it needs to go.

Try paying more attention to how drinking soda affects you. Do you crave it? When you drink soda, do you get a an energy boost for a few minutes followed by a drop in energy a couple hours later? Drinking soda and eating sweets makes you crave more soda and more sweets. The healthier people eat, the fewer sugar cravings they have!

We need to keep our bodies running at their best by not filling our tank with fuel that will damage our insides. You can do this by eating whole grains, which are complex carbohydrates. Whole grains are "whole" because they still have all three parts intact: the germ, bran, and endosperm. When grains are refined (or processed), the germ and bran get removed. This is taking away fiber, antioxidants, and other important nutrients.

Oatmeal, a whole grain and complex carb, takes a longer time to digest in your stomach and intestines, and therefore will keep you full and energized for longer. Other whole grains, like brown rice, whole wheat pasta, whole wheat bread, barley, and quinoa will do the same thing! These complex carbs will help your brain stay on task and supply your body with the tools to repair and function.

Get your good carbs!

• Whole oats: Buy the oats advertised as "five minute oats." Pour them in a bowl with just enough water to barely cover the top and microwave for five minutes. You can add nuts, dried fruit, or milk if you'd like. If you want, dice up some apples and add some cinnamon before you microwave the oats, and you have your very own apple-cinnamon oatmeal, with a fraction of the sugar. David eats oatmeal with a smoothie on top almost every morning.

• Sweet potatoes: These are a complex carb and can be eaten instead of a grain! Wrap these in some tin foil and bake for thirty minutes. These are great to eat with chili and have more vitamins than your regular brown potato.

• Quinoa: This whole grain can be eaten just like rice. This grain has more protein than any other grain. Just take one cup of dried quinoa and two cups of water, and cook at medium heat until it's done.

- Brown rice: If you don't have a rice cooker, get a pot and use two cups of water for every cup of rice. Like quinoa, let it simmer on medium heat until it's done. It should take about thirty minutes.

Try to avoid the simple carbs!

Enriched flour
High fructose corn syrup
High amounts of lactose (milk)
Sugar drinks
White bread
Candy
Potato chips

Veggies: Find them and eat them

According to a CDC survey, nine out of ten teens fail to eat two or more servings of veggies per day. What's so good about vegetables, anyway? They're high in fiber, low in fat, and have lots and lots of vitamins and antioxidants (which help battle diseases). They also tend to be low in calories, but because they're high in fiber, they make us feel full. They will make your heart happy—literally. Eating vegetables protects your arteries, meaning they can help fight against heart disease and other diseases. Not to mention that they're good for your eyes, skin, bones, muscles, and brain too.

Veggies are also a complex carbohydrate, so they are part of your fuel. Again, imagine your body is a car. While veggies act as a fuel, they're also like the coolant fluid. Without coolant your car will overheat and possibly explode. Now, you aren't going to explode if you don't eat vegetables, but you will most likely have a lot of health problems! The vitamins and antioxidants found in veggies protect our body from the stresses we put on it. Vegetables help regenerate damages done to your body (like exercising or eating junk food) and maximize your efforts.

How many vegetables a day do you eat? Do you have a slice of lettuce, tomato, and onion on your sandwich and call it a day? Well, this is equal to using eye drops to put out a fire! We recommend eating at least five servings of veggies per day. This may seem like a lot, but remember, start with baby steps! Whether its breakfast, lunch, dinner, or a snack, grab some baby carrots, sauté some kale, bake some cauliflower, or steam some spinach. Your body will thank you later.

Beginning to eat vegetables can be difficult because you don't know what to do with them. It's easy to eat a raw carrot or microwave some frozen peas, but cooking vegetables can turn into an art, and it's about as difficult as finger painting.

Different veggies have a different thicknesses, so start with one, and get the feel for it. You may want to begin with steaming broccoli. Put a little bit of water in the bottom of a pan, turn the stove on medium heat, and cover with a lid. In a couple minutes, the broccoli will turn a darker green; poke it with a toothpick or a fork to see if it's cooked to your liking. Add a little salt if you'd like, and there you go!

Once you know how to cook a couple vegetables, everything else will become much easier, and you can experiment. Be creative! Like I said, consider this a lifelong process that you will continue to improve at. Some of you have no experience cooking whatsoever. Carolyn and I were both at that point, but we have picked up bits of information here and there: what is healthy, what is not; how to cook this or that. The Internet can be a useful tool. Use it to look up healthy recipes or easy cooking methods.

Preparing a sautéed veggie:

Step one: I always start my veggie dishes by sautéing some freshly diced onions. This means adding a tiny bit of oil to a pan and adding onions. Stir those around for three minutes on medium heat.

Step two: Add the veggie of your choice. Good choices include:

• Kale: a green leafy veggie sold in a bunch. Cut off the stems and chop into edible pieces and add to your pan.

• Zucchini or squash: Cut into half circles, throw into pan.

• Asparagus: Snap off the bottoms (they're hard and chewy) and discard those pieces. Add the good parts to your pan and cook until they're the texture you like!

Step three: Add a little salt and you're done!

Sneaking in raw veggies:

Spinach: Excellent for salads, but I throw this in just about everything. If you get frozen spinach, you can use it over several weeks. You can throw it in smoothies without it affecting the taste very much. You can also easily throw it into a pan with some beans and brown rice.

Carrots: Cut these into thin slices and eat like chips with salsa, guacamole, hummus, or my mixture of beans, rice, and veggies!

Fruits: Getting the real thing

Fruits, like vegetables, are good for you because they're high in vitamins, antioxidants, and fiber. Fructose is the natural sugar found in fruit. It is a simple carbohydrate. So if fruit is made from a simple sugar, how is it good for you? The fiber found in fruit allows the sugar to digest slowly, like a complex carbohydrate. When you process the fruit, all the fiber gets taken away, and all you're left with are some vitamins and antioxidants and a whole lot of sugar.

Fruit should be eaten in its whole form, unprocessed with no added sugars. It's time to realize the difference between eating fruit and "fruit." This means knowing that drinking apple juice is not the same as eating apples, grape jelly is not the same as grapes, and a blueberry bagel does not count as a serving of fruit. And watch out for canned fruit packaged in syrup! Juices, fruit drinks, jellies, jams, fruit snacks, and syrups are full of those simple sugars, with no fiber. **Some fruit juices have more sugar than soda!**

We believe it's best to eat fruit as it comes off the tree. This goes back to the basic concept we are trying to convey, that food was intended to be eaten in its most natural form. This can be difficult because the food industry really screws things up. When food gets processed it usually loses all its fiber and a lot of nutrients. Fiber has many health benefits. It does much more than increase the number of times you use the restroom. It also reduces your cholesterol by attaching to cholesterol in your intestines and bringing it out of your body. Fiber is found in all plant foods. It's not in meat, and is found in trace amounts in processed foods.

Eating real fruit:

Buy frozen fruit (or freeze it yourself). You can get berries, mangoes, or bananas. Add these together with some low-fat yogurt or milk and voila! You have a delicious snack or dessert. There is no right combination. You can use any mixture of fruit.

• Cut apples into thin slices and dip them in plain yogurt.

• Slice up oranges and have them after a workout for some quick energy.

• Pre-wash and slice any fruit and put it in a clear container, so it's ready to eat whenever you want a snack.

Protein:

Proteins are made up of amino acids, which make up the machinery of our body. Protein gets a lot of publicity, but in reality most Americans are eating too much protein and from unhealthy sources. The average person needs 0.8 grams of protein per kilogram of body weight per day. So if you weigh 120 lbs, you need 54 grams of protein a day.
Try it for yourself!

Your weight: _____/2.2=_____kg.
Your weight in kg:_____x0.8=_____ grams of protein.

When you think of protein, you probably think of a big, juicy steak! This is understandable because our society emphasizes eating "high-quality" or "complete" proteins. A high-quality protein means that it contains all of the amino acids we need to build muscle and function at full capacity. High-quality proteins are meat, dairy, and eggs. However, you can get protein from plant foods! Unfortunately, high-protein plant foods are labeled "low-quality" or "incomplete" proteins, making them appear inferior to meat, dairy, and eggs.

David and I get most of our protein from beans, lentils, nuts, and whole grains like quinoa. We prefer plant protein because when you eat beans, lentils, and nuts, not only are you getting protein, but you are also getting fiber and antioxidants! So whole grains, nuts, beans, lentils, and some vegetables are all "low-quality" proteins, but when you're eating them throughout the day, your body gets all of the amino acids it needs to sustain your body. Edamame (soybeans) and quinoa are often considered to be high-quality proteins!

There are some protein sources you should be leery of. Any meat high in fat or cholesterol should be avoided. This means staying away from anything breaded and deep fried (fried chicken), bacon, lobster, shrimp, and beef. You should also avoid processed meat like spam and beef jerky; these are high in sodium and preservatives that aren't good for your body. Processed soy products are also high in sodium and should be eaten with caution! Good sources of animal protein are Greek yogurt, eggs, cottage cheese, salmon, tuna, turkey, or chicken.

Protein supplements are not necessary if you plan in such a way to get protein from your diet. If you are determined to lift weights to "bulk up," your protein needs increase to 1.3-1.8 grams of protein per kilogram of body weight. So if you are a 170-pound male, at most you would need 100 to 140 grams of protein a day.

Regarding brain health, we have discussed that complex carbohydrates provide the fuel for your brain to function over the course of the day, but another important component of brain health is the amino acid tryptophan. Amino acids are the building blocks of proteins in your body, but tryptophan can also act as two important molecules that help you feel happy and fall asleep. Tryptophan in the brain becomes serotonin, an important neurotransmitter that has been linked to how you feel. Tryptophan also becomes melatonin, which helps you fall asleep at night. Thus when starved of tryptophan we can have problems sleeping and feeling good. The best way to get good amounts of tryptophan is to eat it with carbs which moves it into the brain. Good sources of protein that are rich, dense, and full of tryptophan are: tofu, sesame seeds, almonds, walnuts and ground flax seed.

How to get protein in your day:

• Breakfast: 1 medium sized apple, 1.5 cups multigrain Cheerios, 1 cup soy milk

• Lunch: tuna sandwich (3 oz. tuna, 2 slices of whole wheat bread, spinach, tomato and onion), 15 baby carrots and 2 tbsp. of hummus, and 1 cup of grapes

• Dinner: 1 medium baked potato, 1 cup kidney beans, 1.5 cups of broccoli, and ¼ cup of almonds or walnuts

That gives you about 1,800 calories and a whopping 90g of protein! If you're female, 1,800 calories is probably enough for you; if you're male, you may need more calories. You can add snacks in between meals or make fruit and veggie-filled smoothies. Remember to listen to your body. Eat if you're hungry, and stop eating when you're full.

How to cook beans:

Beans (black beans, kidney beans, garbanzo beans, pinto beans): These can be bought in a can, but I recommend eventually learning how to cook them from dried beans. Take a couple cups of dried beans, put them in a bowl of water, and let them soak overnight. The next day, when you want to eat them, drain them and let them simmer in a pot for one to three hours with salt to taste. While they boil, you can throw in spices to make the beans rich in flavor. I recommend cumin, cayenne pepper, and black pepper. Try different combinations and different cooking times until you get something you love. Truly, you can save a ton of money by cooking your beans yourself.

Fats: Nuts, seeds, and oil

Fat. It really isn't as bad as it sounds, I promise. Fat is really good for you, as long as it's coming from a plant source. Fat is important for your energy stores, cell function, brain power, hormones, vitamin absorption, and, yes, insulation. Everyone needs fat!

There are different types of fat: saturated fat, trans fat, monounsaturated fat (MUFA), and polyunsaturated fat (PUFA). In general, you want to decrease your saturated and trans fat. This means switching from whole milk to skim milk (or soy), skipping the butter, choosing lean meats like chicken breast, and avoiding fried food. Trans fat is hidden in processed food as a way to prolong the life of the food, but it is not processed naturally by your body. Read your labels! Next time you see "partially hydrogenated oil" or "trans fat," put that box back on the shelf. Even if the nutrition label says "0g trans fat," there may still be partially hydrogenated oil in the ingredients.

Saturated and trans fat are the fats that give fat a bad rap. These fats can damage your blood vessels, raise your cholesterol, and make you more susceptible to multiple diseases.

The fats you want to eat are your MUFAs and PUFAs. Within your PUFAs you have your omega-3s. These are essential fatty acids—essential because your body does not produce them, and therefore you must get them in your diet to function properly.

If your body was a car, then good fat would be the oil that keeps everything running smoothly. Don't be afraid of fat! Remember what we've been saying: food should come from its most natural source, and fat is no exception. Natural healthy fats can be found in nuts like almonds, pecans, walnuts, and cashews; seeds like sunflower seeds, flax seeds, pumpkin seeds, and sesame seeds; olives; and avocados.

Over 66% of Americans are overweight, so we must be getting enough fat, right? Wrong. Americans are getting too much of the bad fats, and not enough of the good fats. Americans don't get nearly enough of omega-3 fatty acids, which, as I said earlier are a type of PUFA. Omega-3s help with brain function and protect the lining of your blood vessels, making your heart happy and healthy. Studies have shown that people who have severe depression, bipolar disorder, or schizophrenia have lower omega-3 content in their brain.

Here are some foods whose fats have the highest omega-3 content per weight:

Walnuts
Ground flaxseed
Soybeans (tofu, soymilk)

Spinach
Almonds
Avocados
Real olives
Occasional use of olive oil or canola oil
Hummus
Fish (highest: Atlantic Mackerel > Shad Fillet > Halibut > Herring > Salmon)

Fats to never eat:

Trans-fatty acids, partially hydrogenated fatty acids

Fats to eat rarely if at all:

Animal fat (like cheese, cream, meat fat), oil, deep fried foods

Eating too much fat will make you gain weight, but so will eating too much protein or too many complex carbs. It's important to get the right amount of everything you eat. Listen to your body. Eat when you're hungry, and stop when you're full. Eating the right portion sizes is where Americans have the biggest problem. Ever eat a meal that makes you feel very tired afterward? This happens when you've eaten too much. All the food in your stomach draws blood away from your brain and down to your digestive system. Meal timing and size also affects your well-being. We try to eat a big breakfast, a moderate-sized lunch and a smaller dinner. Eating late at night disturbs your sleep!

Concluding Thoughts:

We want you to live life to its fullest. When you fill your body with healthy, unprocessed food, you will feel good and energized! We have laid out these concepts for you to maximize your brain and body function. Fill your body with whole food and stay away from processed food!

Some of your thoughts may be similar to ours when we first went through this process: I don't even know how to cook; all I eat are processed foods; I could never make changes like that; I don't have the resources to make those changes. The last thing we want is for you to feel discouraged. Take baby steps and be encouraged, because we are here to help you!

If you see these tips as things to work toward, to explore and to be curious about, then you can progressively move toward a more healthy approach to eating. Start where you feel comfortable! I think if you make small changes that you keep for the rest of your life, you will be your ideal body weight, happy, and able to concentrate and move one step closer to achieving your maximum potential.

It is so important for you to eat healthy food because we don't want you to be the typical American, who is overweight and suffers from heart disease or diabetes. Obesity, heart disease, and diabetes are serious threats to Americans. More people die of type 2 diabetes and heart disease every day than in wars overseas, yet we don't see it the same way because the death is not immediate, and most Americans do not realize that their lifestyle is influencing the quality and longevity of their lives. Remember: this is not a diet, but a blessing! Eating healthy will change your body from the inside out. Healthy choices make happy people. You can do it!

Now that you have learned to eat healthier, share what you have learned with whoever does the cooking in your home. Here is your chance to change not only your diet, but the diet of your entire household to a much healthier one.

"My Life My Power provides the tools necessary to have a long and healthy life. This world is but a canvas to your imagination."

—Skye Stevens, Recording Artist, Dancer, Writer, and Producer

Chapter 15

LIFESTYLE

by David Puder, M.D.

You have many choices that will deeply change your course in life. This section provides powerful tools that will enhance your life. The topics below will be discussed:

- How being curious can make learning about life rich and enjoyable

- How to go about picking good friends that will last a lifetime

- How what you put in your mind will influence your behavior

- How sleep plays an important role in your performance

Let yourself be curious!

When I was a third-year medical student, I read an amazing article on curiosity. It talked about how scientists found that the students who took the most literature, history, and other non-science classes in college became the best doctors down the road. Subsequently, medical schools required more non-science classes because they thought this was going to help their students become better doctors. But instead, it caused doctors to become burned out! They were wrong. After further investigation, it became clear that the reason some doctors were taking more classes outside of their chosen career was because they were curious. Their curiosity led them to look into all areas of life. The people who were presented with something they did not understand, continued to search for answers and turned out to be more successful because they were lifelong learners. Ideally, our approach to life should be one that is driven by a continual curiosity.

Why is curiosity so powerful? Curiosity is what will lead you down the path of discovery. Do you feel a desire to know more, to discover the reason? Good! This is the beginning of curiosity.

One time, I had a patient who lost his ability to move his eyes (they were frozen looking straight ahead) and who was very clumsy like he was drunk. No one knew what was going on with him. I opened up my internet search engine and found out that eyes frozen in place was termed "ophthalmoplegia" and his clumsiness was termed "ataxia." I did a search on the two things and found several diseases that could cause these symptoms. As I continued to read, one of them came to my attention as the thing that made the most sense, and I was right! My curiosity saved his life, as we knew exactly how to treat him.

We need to let our curiosity grow every day. If you stay open and let your mind go, you will be passionately excellent. Why? Let's say I was a curious doctor that continued to search for answers all my life and this led me to read one book per week. In ten years I would have read 520 more books than a person who is not curious. I know several doctors who never stopped learning. They are so far beyond everyone else, I cannot explain it in words. To be around them is to be in the presence of a master.

In your school classes, you will come upon many things you do not understand. Be curious and find answers. Here are some practical ways that I found my curiosity could make me an excellent student:

• When first opening a book, read the table of contents and allow yourself to be curious

• When reading a chapter of a book, first quickly skim the chapter for the titles and pictures of the different portions, then be curious about the subject material

• When doing homework or class work, if there is something you do not understand or have a question about, write it out

• Try to find answers by looking at other books or doing online searches

• Find time to go over questions you have with the teacher after class or when they are available to meet

What are you curious about today?

_____

_____

What from your reading in class today made you think, "I wonder why? I wonder how?"

_____

_____

If you have these questions, get motivated and find out! If you do this all your life then you will continue to learn and search for truth!

Choosing your friends with a purpose

After transferring to Live Oak High School in Morgan Hill, California, in tenth grade, I remember being the new big guy on campus (I was 6 foot 5 inches and 210 pounds). I was good at football, which surrounded me with new friends. I remember standing around at lunch with the "really-really cool guys." They were talking about foolish things, and I was thinking, "I don't think I will know any of these guys in ten years." Time to find some real friends. I ended up becoming friends with two guys who may not have been the "coolest" but they were the type of people you want to be friends with: dependable, goal-oriented, planning on going to college or doing something big with their lives, and eager to be friends. They also had values, did not bully and were willing to talk about deeper things.

A good friend will be with you through thick and thin. A bad friend will bring you down and not be there for you when you need help. Friends are built on common interests. As you read through this book, you may start to realize things you believe in and want to move toward. Maybe it is college or having a successful career, maybe it will be getting involved in some faith group or a specific sport. My close friends share common values and we hold each other accountable. I choose my friends wisely, and they bring me up when I am down. Good friends are there for you when you need them.

You may need to end some friendships if they are too destructive. You will become like the people you hang out with. If you hang out with people headed toward jail, it's likely you will also head that route (without even knowing it). You may need to recreate your friend group. You may need to humble yourself and work hard to find a good friend. When you meet new people, find out common things that link you together.

Here is what to look for in a friend:

- Someone with whom you have common goals

- Someone who has time to be your friend

- Someone you enjoy being around

- Someone who has good morals

- Someone who enjoys things you enjoy

When you find someone who is good "friend material," pursue them as a friend! Ask them to hang out sometime and do something you both enjoy.

What you put into your mind matters!

Did you know that those who watch more television and have increased total media exposure are more prone to feeling down, hurting others, and spending less time with family and friends? In this section, I am going to present the idea that what you put into your eyes and ears has been shown to have a powerful impact on your own thoughts and actions.

I grew up watching television and playing video games, but in high school I started getting so busy I basically would watch a maximum of an hour or two every week. I love a good movie, and think that some television is worth watching; however, I would like to present some information to you which might be shocking:

• The average American child spends more than 21 hours per week watching television

• At this rate, young people view 10,000 acts of violence per year

• These violent acts are usually without pain, done by attractive people, and often humorous and have become more frequently mixed with sexual content

• In South Africa, the television was introduced in 1975, and between then and 1987, the homicide rate went up 130%

• One author, Centerwall, came up with the estimate that if the television had never been developed, there would be 10,000 fewer murders in the U.S. each year, 70,000 fewer rapes and 700,000 fewer assaults

• Music also has a high percentage of content concerning aggression, drugs, and other high-risk behaviors. In one study on a psychiatric ward, by simply taking off one of the most violent and sexual channels, MTV, the assaultive events went down from forty-four per week to twenty-seven per week!

I could list hundreds more studies, but the basic idea is that what you watch and listen to affects you on a deep level, and most of us are blind to that. If we want to reduce bullying, violence, and other high-risk behaviors and promote more well-being in our youth, we must advocate against media that would promote such things and encourage our audience to spend their time working toward their goals, doing exercise, reading, and moving toward things that will help them thrive!

I find that people often put their "shows" ahead of hanging out with friends and family. Many families eat dinner together while watching television, which makes any meaningful conversations close to impossible.

Approximately 90% of communication is non-verbal, so if you are not watching the person, you are missing what is said, if anything is said at all. Many fathers seem to know more about their sports teams than what is going on in their children's lives. When asked, however, which one is more important, most people will say friends and family. When watching television, due to the rapid movements, camera angle changes, and flashing lights, there is a dissociative effect similar to over eating or drinking alcohol. It has been described as a form of hypnotism that turns down your executive functioning area, the frontal lobe of your brain. When you are in this state of mind, it is hard to filter what is being fed to your brain, and media therefore deeply affects how you think and feel, and even your behaviors. Hence why companies pay millions of dollars to have a thirty second spot in between shows! Also important to understand: when you are disassociating like this, it is impossible to process what you are actually going through in your life; it only delays the period of time when you will have to process things. Thus many of these things become addicting, in that once you stop them you have to find positive things to replace them. The goal of this program is to help you realize what you want out of life, and remove some of the things that may distract you from achieving your goals.

An old saying goes, "Guard your heart, because it is a wellspring of life," meaning be careful what you let into your eyes, ears, mind and thoughts!

How many hours a week to you spend on media (games, TV, movies, social networks)?

_____

Do you ever notice yourself being impacted by what you watch or hear?

_____

How might spending too much time taking in media interfere with your goals?

_____
_____
_____

Sleep equals success!

It may sound strange, but sleep can help you succeed; however, few people talk about how to make sleep work to your benefit! As a doctor, I ask every one of my patients how they are sleeping. I know that if I can get them good sleep then they will feel better, think more clearly, be stronger, and more productive.

Why is sleep important for me? In a deep level of sleep, called Rapid Eye Movement (REM) sleep, the neurotransmitters in your brain are regenerated. Neurotransmitters play a very important role in how you think and feel. Have you ever had no sleep for several days and then found yourself feeling grouchy and unable to concentrate? Lack of sleep reduces your ability to function in the same way as alcohol. In both poor sleep and alcohol use, the first thing to go is your ability to know how impaired you really are! Specifically, the part of your brain called the frontal lobe is impaired under the influence of lack of sleep and alcohol. The frontal lobe has been shown to help you make decisions and work out problems in your mind, and also gives you the ability to have compassion and understand what other people are going through.

Sleep also helps your muscles repair. Many of the people I have known who have trained twice a day for the Olympics have told me that they try to sleep ten hours per day! This is smart training and very enjoyable, but takes discipline. Your muscles need to regenerate just like your brain.

There is good science now on how to obtain the optimum amount of sleep. I propose you try to do these things the majority of nights, knowing that once in a while you will have to have a late night.

• Consistently get to bed at the same time (I try to be in bed by 10 p.m. with lights out)

• Consistently wake up at the same time and get activated! (I set my alarm for 6:30 a.m. so I can get a thirty-minute workout first thing in the morning.)

• The hour before you go to sleep, don't do anything that is stressful and try to dim the lights. Things that are stressful or raise a neurotransmitter (called norepinephrine) include watching TV, playing video games, getting into arguments, and cramming in last-minute homework, to name a few.

• Do some form of exercise every day (but not within three hours of sleep)

• Get bright light in your eyes when you wake up

• Ideally, have your bed be a place you only go when you are going to sleep (don't read, study, eat, or watch television in bed)

• Try using a fan or something similar to create white noise if you have loud disturbances going on outside your house

• Avoid drinking alcohol (this stops you from going into REM sleep)

- Do not take in caffeine after noon (this inhibits sleep even if you don't realize it)

- If you cannot sleep, rather than worrying about not sleeping, get out of bed and read or do something in a different place for twenty minutes and then try to sleep again

- If you are still having problems sleeping after doing all these things, make sure you see a doctor

"Every job, no matter how small it seems, has your signature on it. Make it count. Following the steps in My Life My Power will create a brand you can be proud of."

— Brooke Adams, member of BG5 and TV Personality

Chapter 16

BUILDING YOUR BRAND: RESUME TIPS

by Jackson Wong

What is Personal Branding?

"Personal branding" is a phrase used to describe the process in which you market yourself as a brand. Things like self-improvement, professional success, self-packaging, personal and professional behavior, accomplishments—all these elements are aimed at improving or affecting the impression you make on others. What you do, how you do it, and what you have done can all be part of your own personal branding. This can affect how you are perceived by those you surround yourself with, your present or future employers, and the world. Simply put, **your personal brand is your reputation.**

Working and aspiring professionals are always fine-tuning and shaping their personal brand. When you think about it, every new skill you learn or information you come across can be used to better yourself and be added to your personal brand. It's the constant molding of who you are that makes you a better individual and will help you become a valuable contributor in whatever you do. For you career-minded individuals, you should focus on the talents and the skills you bring to the table. This kind of branding will go hand in hand with your professional resume.

If you applied for a job today, how do you think your potential employers would perceive you as a candidate for a position? Besides making yourself look good on paper, you also have to be aware of how you are as a person outside of work. I'm not talking about your private life, but I am referring to your online profile(s) and presence. Now more than ever, your online persona is as much who you are in person, and employers nowadays screen their candidates by reviewing their online information in addition to their resume and professional references. What you post online will be associated with who you are!

Keep in mind: employers do not know who you are. They have to decide if you are the right candidate to bring on to their team. Your online activity, whether it's on Facebook, Twitter, or other social media sites can make or break your chances of getting hired. You have to be diligent in tracking your own activity and ensure what you post is what you want the world to see. You don't want something you thought was cute or funny to come back to haunt you. Think of all the people you hear about in the news who are denied a position or forced to resign from their jobs due to what they posted on a social network. As unfortunate as it may sound, this is the world we now live in. So wise up!

Experiment: Google yourself. What information can employers or people in general find out about you on the web?

_____

_____

Personal branding comes in many forms and can be anything that is attributed to creating a public profile for yourself. The content that you publish is the most important aspect of how you're able to convey the person you are and the types of skills or talents you possess.

Name a public figure or celebrity that you admire. Describe that individual's personal brand. How would you describe that individual? What are the attributes of his/her brand?

Name of Individual: _____

1. _____
2. _____
3. _____

Activity:

In one or two sentences, how would you describe yourself?

_____

_____

What do others think of you?

_____

_____

What are your best friends or close friends like?

_____

_____

What kinds of people do you surround yourself with?

_____

_____

How should you dress yourself during an interview? (Clothing, shoes, etc.)

_____

_____

What type of jewelry do you want to wear to an interview?

_____

_____

How do you style your hair for an interview?

_____

_____

What kind of first impression do you want to make on someone you just met?

_____

_____

What kinds of people do you want to be associated with?

_____

_____

When you have a conversation with someone, how do you act and how do you use your words?

_____

_____

At a nice dinner, do you know how to use silverware and use proper etiquette, and/or how do you want to be perceived?

_____

_____

How do you shake hands with someone? When you shake someone's hand, is your handshake light, medium, or strong? Do you make eye contact?

_____

_____

When on a date, do you open the door for a woman? If you're a woman, once the man has opened your door and you are seated, do you reach across the seat to open your date's door from the inside?

_____

_____

If you're not sure about the answers to these questions, go to www.MyLifeMyPower.org to access our informational videos for these and other scenarios.

Your ability to sell yourself on paper can be as important as how you sell yourself in person. In recent years, the term "personal branding" has become popular in describing how an individual markets or sells oneself to others. In sports, athletes brand themselves on paper through their own statistical sheet. These stats are very important since they are used to compare and consider candidates for sports teams, ad campaigns, income on contracts, sponsors, etc. For business and working professionals, there are many tools associated with personal branding, and the most important one when applying for a position is the resume.

Experiences

So what should your resume include? A resume should sum up all your experiences and skills in no more than two pages. Under employment history or work experience, you can include past positions in any working environment, internships, and even volunteer work. What you add will help define the amount of overall professional experience you have. For high school students, a resume may not include much in regards to work experience. Therefore, it may be highly important to list and describe the type of leadership, internship, volunteer, or unpaid work you have performed, the results, and the technical skills you have acquired through that work. Such experiences can include volunteering for church functions, tutoring at the local library, duties performed for a school's play production, or leadership functions for a school club or event. Anything you can include to demonstrate the level of leadership or management abilities you have and the skills you've acquired will certainly add points in your overall presentation of your resume.

Volunteering is one of those things that is not only highly rewarding on a personal level, it looks great on a resume as well. If you spend a few hours every week on average helping at a food bank or soup kitchen, include when you first started and the skills you've learned. Perhaps you went abroad and volunteered in a developing country by helping to build houses or aid in the care of less fortunate children. Giving your time and effort to charity without asking for anything in return is something that resonates on a human level. That kind of work is something that is encouraged by almost all employers and it truly demonstrates how well-rounded a candidate you are. For the college-bound, which all of you should be, countless scholarships are awarded to recipient students who demonstrate altruism and self-sacrifice through volunteer work. These kinds of awards can also be added to your resume.

As you move on with other work or change to a new professional environment, those changes will apply to your resume. It's always good to keep in mind that your resume is a tool, and that tools need to be sharpened and kept ready for future opportunities. You should always place your most recent employment or work experience at the top of this section. You then make note of the skills and accomplishments you have acquired to demonstrate to your future employer your career path and your qualifications as a candidate.

Skills: Hard and Soft

Skills are equally as important as experience on a resume, because they help quantify and qualify the abilities you are bringing to your potential employer. As a former hiring manager, I often used the term "skill set" to describe the total package of skills a candidate brings to the table that will enhance my team. Believe it or not, employers do think of their workplace as a "team" setting. These employers tend to look for "hard" skills and "soft" skills that a candidate possesses to help their business grow.

Hard skills or technical skills can be important factors in qualifying a candidate for an open position. Using retail as an example, these hard skills can include being register trained, computer skills, typed words per minute, stockroom experience, etc. These skills may be apparent in your work experience, but it's also good to note them when applying for a position in which these skills come in handy.

Soft skills are talents that are not apparent on paper and cannot be quantified by any measurable means. Many personality and ability traits fall into this category. Again using retail as an example, such skills would include being personable, customer service oriented, having strong organizational and communication skills, being passionate about helping others, the ability to learn or adapt quickly to new skills or situations, time management, etc. Hard and soft skills work hand in hand to produce an image of the skill set a potential candidate will offer an employer.

On a resume, these are noted in a summary either in a short paragraph or a few bullet points, usually at the top of the resume before your work experience. The purpose of the summary is to make a quick highlight of all the core knowledge and skills that make you an ideal candidate for the position you are applying for.

List some of your skills:

HARD SKILLS   **SOFT SKILLS**

1._____ 2._____

3._____ 4._____

5._____ 6._____

Strengths

A major part of your resume should resemble a catalogue of your strengths. Strengths come in many different forms. You may be technically savvy and so computer literate that you can create and design websites. Your technical expertise on computers can be considered a strength. For those aspiring to be writers, your journalistic background and ability to frame words into sophisticated thought can also be considered a strength.

If you don't have strengths in a hard skill, you may have soft skills that can be touted as strengths. Perhaps you have a talent for thinking outside the box that can be harnessed into a solutions-driven strength. One great strength is leadership. Leadership is one of those strengths that can be transferred to any position in any industry. It easily encompasses a bunch of other skills, such as management, resourcefulness, problem-solving, and numerous other subsets of soft skills. In high school and through college, there's plenty of room to develop your leadership abilities, through participation in on-campus clubs and activities, sports, volunteer work, etc. Whatever strengths you possess, your resume needs to speak about those strengths in a cohesive presentation to your future employer.

What are six of your strengths?

1._____ 2._____
3._____ 4._____
5._____ 6._____

When writing your resume, frame the thought and overall theme to these strengths. Make sure that these strengths are pertinent to the position you are applying for.

Interests and Activities

If you are passionate about sports and have been participating on a team for a long period of time, definitely include this on your resume. Employers are highly receptive to team players, and by being on a sports team, your "team-player" qualities should be more apparent. This part of the resume should not overshadow all the skills and experiences you have put forth in previous sections. Things you should include are your participation in school organizations or clubs, any leadership positions, and interests (art, music, photography, etc.) that demonstrate your overall character. This section will help to define what your passions are and who you are as a person outside of work. Employers want to like you as an individual and will try to imagine how well you can integrate into their work team.

What are your interests/activities?

1._____ 2._____
3._____ 4._____

Honors and Achievements

Who doesn't like to shine? This part of the resume is your chance to really focus on your awards, whether in competition or through academics. Perhaps you placed in a debate tournament or academic decathlon, made honor roll every year, or won a trophy for a basketball competition. Congratulations to you! However, much like your interests and activities, keep this section brief. You don't want these accomplishments to be the bulk of your overall resume, since the focus should be on your work experience, not your awards. Most important is how this will provide a picture of who you are as a person, beyond your skills.

List your honors and achievements:

1._____ 2._____
3._____ 4._____
5._____ 6._____

References

References are very important in the employment process. A reference sheet is usually not included in the resume but is usually added as an attachment, given to the employer during an interview, or added at the end of the resume as "references available upon request." In many cases, references can make or break your candidacy. If you list a bunch of your friends as references, chances are your employment potential will drop significantly. Why? Your friends cannot verbally demonstrate your professional abilities with examples. They often lack the knowledge and full understanding of how your skills can be applied in the work environment. That's why it's recommended to keep your references of friends to a maximum of one. Remember, as part of your personal branding, you want to include people that can vouch for both your hard and soft skills in the work place.

How long you've known a particular reference is just as important. For example, if you list a previous supervisor who literally guided you through many positions and promotions within the span of a few years, that reference will be more valuable than, say, a supervisor that you've worked under for only a few months. If you're still in high school or just graduated from high school, perhaps there was a teacher or advisor whom you developed a strong academic relationship with who would be happy to be a reference for you. In some cases, they may even be willing to write you a letter of recommendation. Other potential references may include your sports coach, the school principal, school counselors, club advisors, police officers, supervisors from volunteer projects, etc. Be sure to ask for permission first before including any individual as your reference, so they will know ahead of time and expect a call for your potential employer. Also, as a courtesy, alert your references each time you are informed that they may be contacted.

It's also important to note that you shouldn't include everyone you feel is a person of authority. Perhaps you had a supervisor that didn't like you all that much; that individual may be a bad reference for you. It's always good to maintain a healthy relationship with all those who have a stake in your education or employment. You never know when you might need them for future opportunities to further your career. Most of all, remember that the people you surround yourself with will be an indication of who you are. On a resume, that holds true in the form of your reference sheet.

Who are your top references? (If you have to list a friend, include only one that you have known for a very long time. All others should be teachers, mentors, counselors, advisors, or persons who can speak about your abilities.)

Name	Phone #	Email
1._____ , _____ , _____
2._____ , _____ , _____
3._____ , _____ , _____

Content Should Be Relevant

One very important thing when submitting a resume: keep the content relevant to your potential employer. For example, if I was a hiring manager for a marketing firm with an entry-level marketing position, I wouldn't want to see your resume listing all of the sports events that show your number of wins or describe how you performed wonderfully. To me, it would not be relevant to the open position. Your resume and application may go straight into the "No" pile, and you might not be considered for an interview. In my past hiring positions, I've placed hundreds of applications and resumes in the "No" pile after reviewing what was being submitted. It's a shame because I may have missed a chance to meet some great candidates, but they didn't shine in their resume at all. Employers have to sift through a lot of applications and will filter out all candidates who do not meet the criteria on paper. This may happen to a lot of candidates on the job hunt. When they call to follow up with the employer and see if they reviewed the resume, the employer may often say, "The position has been filled" or they are "still reviewing all candidates" just to brush the individual off.

To stand out above other candidates, make sure that your resume is tailored for the position you are applying for. For the entry-level marketing position, experiences should include work done on ad campaigns, marketing projects, and perhaps demonstrations of leadership that an entry-level marketing associate might have. Maybe you had an innovative way of marketing a school production or event in such a way that sold out all the tickets to the event. Highlight your ability to capitalize on social media helped to drive ticket sales for your school's club fundraiser and resulted in thousands of dollars raised. For a young individual like yourself, you may not have an extensive employment history, so try and list work experience (even if it's volunteer work) and skills that relate to the job description.

Pay attention to the job posting, since it will give you the clues you need to customize your resume. There will usually be a listing of skills and qualifications that need to be met in order to apply. In turn, you should include the experiences, skills, and accomplishments that fit the job description.

Another Thing to Watch Out For

Nothing bothers an employer more than reading a resume that has multiple typos and grammatical errors. If you submit a resume that displays such mistakes, it will demonstrate that you lacked the effort to ensure that you put your best foot forward. A resume is basically your advertisement. It's your personal brand of who you are on paper. You have to make sure your brand is the best compared to all other candidates vying for that position. As the first impression of you as a candidate to your potential employer, you better make sure your resume is the best it can be. Have a teacher, a mentor, or even a friend go through your resume to identify mistakes. Sometimes when you're writing your resume, you may have read it over and over again so many times that those little mistakes get missed.

Don't forget to make sure your name and contact information is correct as well. I've encountered resumes where I could not reach the candidate because they entered their information incorrectly on their resume. These little mistakes can have a huge affect on the outcome of your potential candidacy for employment. With all of the sections in this chapter you have filled out, you can start building your resume on the computer. Look at the layout below and follow this structure as you put your information in.

Sample Resume:

Straight A. Student
Cell | 321-123-4567
Email | Student@mylifemypower.org

EDUCATION_____

- My Life My Power High School, Los Angeles, CA (2008-2012); GPA: 4.0

- College Extension Classes at University, Los Angeles, CA (Summer 2011); GPA: 3.5

- Courses: Biology 1, Advanced Mathematics, Intro to Engineering

SUMMARY_____

- Sales Supervisor with 2+ years experience in retail sales environment and 4 years in overall management

- Self-motivated and energetic, reliable and efficient; quick to learn and adapt; team player

- Core Strengths: Team leadership and delegating skills, mentoring, customer service

- Computer Skills and Programs: Type 50 WPM, Microsoft Excel, Word, PowerPoint

WORK & VOLUNTEER EXPERIENCE_____

SALES SUPERVISOR – Overachievers 'R' Us, Los Angeles, CA, Mar. 2010 & July 2012

- Provided customer experiences that were of the highest satisfaction with personable customer interaction

- Managed register functions, inventory, customer service sales team, and other daily operations

MENTOR – My Life My Power Mentorship Program (Volunteer), MLMP H.S.
Sept. 2010 – June 2012

- Guided incoming freshman through a buddy system and through school and club activities

- Trained new mentors for the MLMP Mentor Program for the next incoming freshmen class

- Organized school fundraisers and events for charity

HOST & MANAGER – Mom and Pop's Pizza, Los Angeles CA Sept. 2008 – Oct. 2010

- Helped to manage overall operations at my family's restaurant

- Maintained quality of both experiences and food to gain loyal patrons and repeat customers

- Trained new employees on job duties and functions

VOLUNTEER – Los Angeles Food Bank, Los Angeles, CA Sept. 2008–Present

- Organized and loaded food items for distribution to local soup kitchens (twice a month)

TUTOR – Local Library, Los Angeles, CA Sept. 2008 – Present

- Helped students with homework on the subjects of biology and math (once a week)

INTERESTS/ACTIVITIES_____

- Sports: Varsity Basketball Team (2011-2012, Point Guard), Varsity Volleyball Team (2010-2012, Outside Hitter)

- Student Council (Vice -President, 2011-2012; Secretary, 2010-2011)

- Member of Yearbook Club, Police Athletics/Activities League (PAL), My   Life My Power Club

HONORS & ACHIEVEMENTS_____
S
- Member of National Honor Society (2008-2012)

- Perfect Attendance (2009-2010, 2010-2011 school year)

- Team Most Valuable Player (Varsity Volleyball, 2011)

- Community Service Scholarship, $1,000 (June 2012)

Not all resumes will look alike. Every individual will have a different set of experiences and skills that make them who they are as a candidate. Consequently, your resume may be structured differently than your friend's. It depends on how you want to present yourself on paper. If you want to review other resume styles, there are a lot of resources online that can help you put together a fantastic resume.

Visit www.MyLifeMyPower.org for helpful resume building tips.

"Financial literacy is not just choosing where you have your checking and savings accounts. Being financially literate can help you control the major events in your life such as, the car you drive, the home you own, and the job you have. Be smart and take control of your financial future now. The earlier you start securing your financial future the more successful you will be."

—Robert York, President and CEO of CAL BEAR Federal Credit Union

DANIEL PUDER

CHAPTER 17:

MONEY 101: STAYING FINANCIALLY FIT

by Jackson Wong

Right after graduation from college was probably the first time I came to the realization that I was in a bit of financial trouble. The word "debt" was not new to me, but it was not part of my everyday financial vernacular. I never quite understood what that meant until I took the time to mentally digest my own personal financial situation. By facing the truth about my situation that I finally became my own personal financial advocate.

Money was not something that I had a personal relationship with, other than me spending and working more so that I can spend more. Money seemed to just appear, even though while in college I worked a total three jobs at one time, to pay for many of my expenses. Every two weeks I'd get a paycheck. In my mind, I thought that money would always be there, coming in that is, and so I didn't need to worry.

Even while growing up, my parents never taught me the value of the dollar other than they had to work so hard for it. Plus, I did not get all the things that I wished for or wanted as a child. From grade school through high school, I did not learn anything about money, and I continued on without a proper education on personal finances. So by the time I reached the age of 18, attended college, and being somewhat independent from my parents, you can say I was pretty naive when it came to money. I felt as though I had the freedom to do whatever I wanted with my money. It was all about hanging out with friends, buying the newest things or gadgets (pagers began dying out and cell phones became super popular at the time), eating out, movies, music (yes, CDs were still in), clothes, etc. = spend, spend, spend. All the things teenagers are stereotypically thought of with regards to consumerism, you can probably check off an entire list with me.

More than 10 years later, I can still do all these things, except I do it with more caution, more knowledge about personal finances. Most of all, I have an ongoing financial plan. As I look back, I wish I'd had a financial mentor or took a class that taught me how to manage my personal finances. There are so many resources now available at my fingertips and I wish I had taken time to prepare myself. Thankfully it wasn't too late and I now understand the financial mistakes I've made while growing up as a teenager and while completing my undergraduate studies. I am more financially fit now than I was five years ago.

The following topics are just some of the financial responsibilities that they don't often teach you in schools.

Checking and Savings

When you start making money, one of the first things you need to do is open a checking account to deposit that money for future use. A checking account at a bank or credit union is a safe way for you to access your money whenever you need it for short-term expenses. Plus you can complete as many transactions as you'd like as long as there are enough funds in the account. What's even more convenient is if your account is linked to a debit card. Once connected, you can use your debit card to pay for everyday purchases like groceries without having to use cash. Nowadays you can even access your account on the web and use it to automatically pay for your bills through your online account. The most common fixed monthly bills may include cell phone services, gym memberships, car payments, rent, and utilities, all of which can now be paid online depending on your preferred banking institution. The important thing with checking accounts is that they are a tool to help you manage your money.

A savings accounts is another secure method of storing your hard earned money. That's why it's called "savings" because you're saving for the future. These future purchases or expenses can be very costly. Some examples are a new car or a new computer. Parents often open a savings account in their child's name to get their children motivated on learning how to save money. Over time, these accounts may graduate into becoming college savings accounts to help ease the burden of college expenses.

There are other important elements to a savings account. Most people generally do not draw from their savings accounts to make large purchases but rather use it as a safety net for any unforeseen emergencies and future expenses (like taxes, car maintenance, or medical expenses). Even more uncommon is kids or young adults having enough money in their savings or even having a savings account at all. You never know when you might need money for emergencies or other expenses. Therefore it's good to get into the habit of putting money into a savings account each month.

The one great thing about a savings accounts is that it will accrue interest over time. The bank will actually pay you a little bit of money in interest for the money you put in a savings account. Imagine that!

It is important to note that your accounts, both checking and savings, are insured by the Federal Deposit Insurance Corporation (FDIC) for bank accounts and the National Credit Union Administration (NCUA) for credit union bank accounts. If something were to happen to your bank or credit union, your accounts and the balances in them will still be safe. This is one of the reasons why it is more secure to store your money in one of these banking institutions than at home. There's no insurance on your money at home if you were to lose it in a robbery.

Credit Cards

Credit cards are probably the most dangerous of the financial mistakes I've made in my early twenties. The first time I got my own credit card was my freshman year back in college while attending UCSD. They were so easy to obtain. To make it even more convenient, credit card companies had my own peers doing fundraisers by getting college students to sign up at Price Center, the main common area on campus where students congregate between classes. All these companies needed was for me to fill out a form on a clipboard and sign. Then I got a free t-shirt or a mug. So I signed up for two!

Up until that point, I'd only seen my parents use their credit cards. I did not fully understand what credit cards meant other than you can borrow money and pay it off later. I was still very much unaware of the value that credit cards hold and how that can affect my overall financial health. All I cared about when I finally got my own was the ability to spend even more. And so I kept spending, thinking that I can just pay a little bit off each month. That mentality prompted me to dig myself into a financial hole. I remember maxing out one credit card and was close to maxing out the other.

The danger lies in the lack of knowledge, and therefore I didn't know what I was getting myself into. Credit cards have their pros and cons-the con for a naive college student was the freedom to spend more than what I needed. Without the proper knowledge of managing the use of credit cards, I ended up with a good amount of debt. There are no easy fixes and the problem was my own to resolve. It took a while for me to pay it off to be financially fit.

Credit cards are issued by credit card companies to their customers, allowing their customers to borrow money on a line of credit. This is very similar to a loan, except there are quite a few elements that make credit cards different from loans. For the average college student and, in some cases, high school students, that line of credit can range anywhere from $500-$1,500 for first time credit card holders. Because of the short credit history or no credit history, card companies are reluctant to issue higher amounts of credit line to younger customers. But knowing that young consumers are more likely to spend, regardless of how fiscally responsible they are, credit cards were at one time handed out like candy.

If you use a credit card, that money is borrowed from the bank that issued you the card. If you cannot repay the bank on time the full amount that you borrowed, the bank charges you interest for borrowing the money. This is one of the ways the banks make their money from credit card usages. This is also how I ended up paying the card companies more each month while in college. Other ways you can get in trouble with credit cards is through convenience fees. For example, say you need cash right away because a merchant doesn't accept credit cards. You find an ATM machine nearby that isn't part of your card or bank's network so you draw money from your card by getting a cash advance. First the company that operates the ATM may charge you a nominal convenience fee. On average it can be anywhere from $1.50 to $3.00. Then your card company will also charge you a convenience fee as well, usually $3.00. On top of that, if you don't pay off the amount you borrowed, the interest charged for cash advances is much higher than regular purchase charges. So you can potentially get hit with three different fees, all for just needing cash right away! Even with debit cards, ATMs that are not part of your bank's network can charge you a convenience fee just for withdrawing money. This is one issue I completely avoided, but it doesn't mean that I didn't do this once or twice. I found this out from reading my card statements.

The best way to utilize credit cards is only for emergencies. If you are financially responsible enough to pay it off in full each month, then maybe you can go ahead and use that card sparingly. However, credit cards should not be your main form of monetary transaction. The amount of credit you use on your credit cards can affect your FICO or credit score. We'll go into that a bit later.

Credit cards have other ways of luring customers besides convenience. They are very good at maintaining loyal customers. I admit, I am one myself. However, I am very responsible about my usage and I make sure I have enough to pay off my balances each month. The way they got me is that banks and credit card companies attach rewards to your account so that you can earn points on every purchase you make. Do be careful not to charge more than you're able to pay off. If you don't have the money, it's better to save up for that purchase. Here's a frame of thought: why should you pay the credit card companies hard-earned money that belongs to you in the first place! So whatever I charge, I pay off right away. In turn, I get the freebies from the rewards, usually in the form of cash deposited to my bank account! Lesson here; take charge and get into the habit of how to use credit cards in a responsible manner.

FICO/Credit Scores

As a teenager and young adult, you're probably most worried about your test scores. And who can blame you? Education is very important and it lays the foundation for your future and your career. In the overall scheme of your financial health, your credit score will become the overall most important factor of your financial being. Why is this so important? And what if my credit score is bad?

A FICO is the most widely used score that determines your credit worthiness as an individual. This score is assigned and monitored by three credit bureaus (Experian, TransUnion, and Equifax) and is calculated based on the likelihood of you paying your debts. When you need to borrow money and apply for a loan, banks and credit unions will utilize this score to evaluate their risk of lending you money. That is why it is important to maintain good or excellent credit. A higher score shows banks and credit unions that you are not a lending risk. In addition to your ability to obtain loans, your FICO score also determines the interest rates you will pay on those loans and the amount of credit you will receive. Credit scores range from 300-850 and to receive those excellent rates, you want to be the mid-700s or higher.

There are a lot of factors that will affect your score, including taking on too much debt when compared to available credit or failing to pay your credit card bills on time. Such actions can adversely affect your score and, in turn, affect your ability to get the best financing options. Simply put, you may end up paying more in interest on a loan or having a loan application denied.

How to Stay Out of Debt

Being in debt is not fun. Believe me. I've been there. It meant that I couldn't go out and eat with my friends as often or go to the movies. Even though I felt like it was a personal sacrifice to miss out on all the good times my friends were having, I had to stay focused on getting myself out of debt. Just because you're in debt, doesn't mean you can't get yourself out from that big financial hole. It really takes time and figuring out ways to cut spending and paying off those bills. For me it meant going out less and managing my expenses better and more frequently.

Two things to remember: be careful of how you use credit cards and don't borrow more money if you can't pay it off immediately. You're basically hedging against your own future financial fitness if you fail to heed these warnings. The thing about money is that once you've earned it, you have to be responsible about how you spend it. It's always easier to spend. That hard-earned money can easily disappear quickly in one single trip to the mall. There will always be new games, new movies, new clothes, new everything. Those purchases can quickly add up. If you use a credit card, you can really get yourself into trouble and rack up debt on all kinds of stuff.

Here's a great tip: start breaking down what it is you need versus what it is you want. You'll begin to realize that there are plenty of things you don't really need, but just want. For example, you have a perfectly good working computer. Do you absolutely need to buy a brand new one? If you already have five pairs of perfectly good shoes, do you need a new pair? Once you figure this out, you'll be smarter on how you spend your money and end up saving more. Simply exercise caution whenever you want to spend on discretionary items. Overall, it's really about how you perceive your own money and your spending habits that will help save you from debt issues.

Spending, Saving, and Investing

Saving money is a great way to prevent yourself from being burdened by debt. It becomes easier once you get into the habit of it. Think of it this way: pay yourself first. What do I mean? For most young adults, once they get a paycheck, they will immediately spend it all and have nothing left for themselves. The money they worked hard for is used to pay for all kinds of things, and the majority will probably be spent on stuff that is not needed. Never do we think of ourselves as a necessary expense. If we shift our attitude about saving and consider it an expense, then the habit of saving just became easier.

Saving can also be considered an investment as well. Investing doesn't have to be about stocks, bonds, or monetary investments. Investing can be about preparing for your future, and the return is a secure financial future for yourself. How much should you be saving or investing in yourself? There are a lot of rules out there that explain how much you should be saving. However, there really isn't a single "correct" rule that everyone should be following. 10%, 15%, or 20% of your income. Those are just nice round numbers you will encounter from people who will tell you how much you should be saving. The truth is, it depends on a lot of different factors which includes your age, your current savings, your income, and years until retirement. The earlier you begin saving, the more you'll end up with when you do retire.

Now, if you are in junior high or high school, you might not exactly be thinking about saving for retirement. Instead, you want to be thinking about saving for college. Maybe you don't have a job yet and are only receiving an allowance from your parents. And if you do have a job, maybe you are already planning to attend college and have begun setting aside money for those expenses. Regardless, its the habit of saving that will help you out in the long run, whether it is to lower the costs of your college education or building your retirement savings.

How to Balance Your Budget

Before you create a budget, you have to know a few things first.

1. How much do you make each month (gross)? What is your take-home pay (net)? _____

2. How much do you spend each month? What is the total of your monthly expenses? _____
_____

3. What are your financial goals (short-term and long-term)?_____
_____

4. What are some things that you want?_____
_____

It's imperative that you examine where your money is going or how your money is spent over the course of each month. When you begin tracking your expenses, you'll realize the amount of money it really takes to fund your current lifestyle. Are you overspending? Are you not saving enough? These are some additional questions that will come up once you figure out your budget.

So let's begin to figure out a simple budget. Start with how much money you make. Assuming you're out of college, living on your own, and you have a secure job, your net monthly take-home income is roughly $3,000. This is after all the taxes have been taken out.

The next step is to figure out your monthly expenses. For fixed expenses, let's say you pay $1,150 for rent every month, $75 for water and utilities, $50 for Internet and cable TV, $80 for your wireless phone bill, $30 for a gym membership, $200 for car payments, $100 for car insurance, $100 for student loan payments, and $100 on medical insurance. That's a total of $1,855 so far. Let's say on top of that, you average about $400 on food and groceries and roughly $200 for transportation or gas to go to work. Perhaps you have other miscellaneous expenses (like credit card bills or entertainment) that total about $100 per month. Grand total for your expenses is $2,535. But wait! You forgot to pay yourself too! So you put about $350 away in a savings account. What's left?

Your total monthly expenses should be subtracted from your monthly net income. In this example, you should have a total of $115 left over for whatever it is you want. You can use this left over money for going out to a nicer dinner once a month or buy yourself some new clothes. Maybe a snowboarding trip in January! Whatever it is, you want to make sure you have some money left over to treat yourself. Or you can put this money away in another savings account and start building up the funds to take a nice vacation or buy something nice that you've always wanted.

Here is how this budget would look:

SAMPLE

Monthly Net Income (Take Home)	$3000

EXPENSES

- Rent $1150
- Water & Utilities $75
- Cable & Internet $50
- Cellular Phone $80
- Gym Membership $30
- Car Payments & Insurance $300
- Student Loans $100
- Medical Insurance $100
- Food & Groceries $400
- Transportation (Gas) $200
- Other (Entertainment, credit cards) $100
- Savings $35

TOTAL EXPENSES	**$2885**
Monthly Net Income – Total Expenses	$115

After creating your budget, what are your financial goals? Do you want to have a stable retirement? Do you want to go on a vacation? Do you want a new car? Maybe there's some debt you want to pay down. Maybe you want to cut costs to some of your expenses so you end up saving more money for discretionary expenditures. These are some goals you want think about once you have a clearer grasp of your financial situation and you can begin factoring these goals into your monthly budget.

A monthly budget is a great tool to help you visualize where exactly your money is going. The most important thing is when you do create your own budget, is to have a plan in place with some specific goals in mind. For me, it was to buy a new car. Before I can do that, I needed to save up a lot of money for a down payment and increase my FICO score by paying down my debt first. After paying down my debt and saving for the car, I also included paying myself by putting money away in an online savings account and having money taken out from my paychecks and placed in my employer's 401(k) funds. Eventually with the additional funds left over, I increased my "self" payments by saving more and opening up an IRA account to boost my overall retirement savings. Having these plans in place really established a habit of saving for me that have become an active part of my overall financial fitness, and I still had money left over to do whatever it is I wanted!

YOUR PERSONAL BUDGET

Monthly Net Income (Take Home)   _____

EXPENSES

Rent	_____
Water & Utilities	_____
Cable & Internet	_____
Cellular Phone	_____
Gym Membership	_____
Car Payments & Insurance	_____
Student Loans	_____
Medical Insurance	_____
Food & Groceries	_____
Transportation (Gas)	_____
Other (Entertainment, credit cards)	_____
Savings	_____
TOTAL EXPENSES	_____
Monthly Net Income – Total Expenses	_____

Available Resources

There are a number of online resources you can use to learn more about money and personal finances that are dedicated to the financial well being of anyone who has an interest in helping themselves become more financially fit.

Check out www.MyLifeMyPower.org

APPENDIX A

QUIZ BEFORE YOU READ THE BOOK

MY LIFE MY POWER QUIZ

Take the following quiz before you read this book to see how many exciting tips and facts you will learn.

1) From Chapter #1: Have you ever written down what you like and dislike?

A. Yes B. No

2) From Chapter #2: Do you have a mentor you look up to in your life?

A. Yes B. No

3) From Chapter #3: Have you ever set short-term and long-term goals?

A. No B. Yes

4) From Chapter #4: Do you know what your biggest fears are and the consequences of not overcoming these fears?

A. No B. Yes

5) From Chapter #5: Do you know how to turn your past failures into successes?

A. Yes B. No

6) From Chapter #6: Do you know the breakdown of the amount of time you spend each day on each of your daily activities?

A. Yes B. No

7) From Chapter #7: Do you have a time line as to how you will achieve your life's goals? Do you know exactly why you want to achieve your goals?

A. Yes B. No

8) From Chapter #8: Do you know what motivates you to improve your overall health and feelings of well-being?

A. Yes B. No

9) From Chapter #9: Have you ever been taught how to work out your problems with other people?

A. Yes B. No

10) From Chapter #10: Have you ever done charity work?

A. Yes B. No

11) From Chapter #11: Do you know the six steps to being a leader?

A. No B. Yes

12) From Chapter #12: Do you know the ways that bullying can impact other people?

A. Yes B. No

13) From Chapter #13: Have you been taught the importance of exercise?

A. Yes B. No

14) From Chapter #14: Have you ever been educated about nutrition and how to eat?

A. No B. Yes

15) From Chapter #15: Have you ever been taught the importance of sleep?

A. No B. Yes

16) From Chapter #16: Do you have a resume?

A. Yes B. No

17) From Chapter #17: Do you have a bank account?

A. Yes B. No

APPENDIX B

QUIZ AFTER YOU READ THE BOOK

MY LIFE MY POWER QUIZ

Take the following quiz after you read this book to see how many exciting tips and facts you have learned.

1) From Chapter #1: Have you ever written down what you like and dislike?

A. Yes B. No

2) From Chapter #2: Do you have a mentor you look up to in your life?

A. Yes B. No

3) From Chapter #3: Have you ever set short-term and long-term goals?

A. Yes B. No

4) From Chapter #4: Do you know what your biggest fears are and the consequences of not overcoming these fears?

A. Yes B. No

5) From Chapter #5: Do you know how to turn your past failures into successes?

A. Yes B. No

6) From Chapter #6: Do you know the breakdown of the amount of time you spend each day on each of your daily activities?

A. Yes B. No

7) From Chapter #7: Do you have a time line as to how you will achieve your life's goals? Do you know exactly why you want to achieve your goals?

A. Yes B. No

8) From Chapter #8: Do you know what motivates you to improve your overall health and feelings of well-being?

A. Yes B. No

9) From Chapter #9: Have you ever been taught how to work out your problems with other people?

A. Yes B. No

10) From Chapter #10: Have you ever done charity work?

A. Yes B. No

11) From Chapter #11: Do you know the six steps to being a leader?

A. Yes B. No

12) From Chapter #12: Do you know the ways that bullying can impact other people?

A. Yes B. No

13) From Chapter #13: Have you been taught the importance of exercise?

A. Yes B. No

14) From Chapter #14: Have you ever been educated about nutrition and how to eat?

A. Yes B. No

15) From Chapter #15: Have you ever been taught the importance of sleep?

A. Yes B. No

16) From Chapter #16: Do you have a resume?

A. Yes B. No

17) From Chapter #17: Do you have a bank account?

A. Yes B. No

WEEKLY PLANNER

Remember that one of the keys to success is to develop and maintain a well-rounded, healthy lifestyle. An easy way to be successful at this, is to journal the entire process until you are able to build a steady routine. It is important to keep track of the amount of water that you drink, what you eat, the amount of sleep that you get each night, and your daily homework and chores so that you can be as productive as possible. It is these factors that will positively challenge you toward balancing your healthy lifestyle and achieving your goals in life.

This weekly planner provided in this book is an excellent tool, which can be used as your own personal checklist. So be sure to keep track of all daily activities, and you will be on your way to a healthy and successful life.

WEEK:_____/_____/20_____

MONDAY   I'm feeling: ☺ ☺ ☺ ☹ ☹ ☹

		Due Date
Class #1	_____	_____
Class #2	_____	_____
Class #3	_____	_____
Class #4	_____	_____
Class #5	_____	_____
Class #6	_____	_____
Class #7	_____	_____

Meals   Water 8oz   Snacks   Water 8oz
1_____ ☐ 1_____ ☐
2_____ ☐ 2_____ ☐
3_____ ☐ Responsibilities, Chores, Homework ☐

TUESDAY   I'm feeling: ☺ ☺ ☺ ☹ ☹ ☹

		Due Date
Class #1	_____	_____
Class #2	_____	_____
Class #3	_____	_____
Class #4	_____	_____
Class #5	_____	_____
Class #6	_____	_____
Class #7	_____	_____

Meals   Water 8oz   Snacks   Water 8oz
1_____ ☐ 1_____ ☐
2_____ ☐ 2_____ ☐
3_____ ☐ Responsibilities, Chores, Homework ☐

WEDNESDAY I'm feeling: ☺ ☺ ☺ ☹ ☹ ☹

		Due Date
Class #1	_____	_____
Class #2	_____	_____
Class #3	_____	_____
Class #4	_____	_____
Class #5	_____	_____
Class #6	_____	_____
Class #7	_____	_____

Meals   Water 8oz   Snacks   Water 8oz
1_____ ☐ 1_____ ☐
2_____ ☐ 2_____ ☐
3_____ ☐ Responsibilities, Chores, Homework ☐

WEEK: _____/_____/20_____

THURSDAY I'm feeling: ☺ 😐 😕 ☹ 😣 😫

		Due Date
Class #1 _____		_____
Class #2 _____		_____
Class #3 _____		_____
Class #4 _____		_____
Class #5 _____		_____
Class #6 _____		_____
Class #7 _____		_____

Meals	Water 8oz	Snacks	Water 8oz
1_____	☐	1_____	☐
2_____	☐	2_____	☐
3_____	☐	Responsibilities, Chores, Homework	☐

FRIDAY I'm feeling: ☺ 😐 😕 ☹ 😣 😫

		Due Date
Class #1 _____		_____
Class #2 _____		_____
Class #3 _____		_____
Class #4 _____		_____
Class #5 _____		_____
Class #6 _____		_____
Class #7 _____		_____

Meals	Water 8oz	Snacks	Water 8oz
1_____	☐	1_____	☐
2_____	☐	2_____	☐
3_____	☐	Responsibilities, Chores, Homework	☐

SATURDAY ☺ 😐 😕 ☹ 😣 😫   **SUNDAY** ☺ 😐 😕 ☹ 😣 😫

Responsibility, Chores, Homework ☐	Responsibility, Chores, Homework ☐
_____	_____
_____	_____
_____	_____
_____	_____

GOALS

Weekly _____

_____

Monthly _____

_____

WEEK:_____/_____/20_____

MONDAY I'm feeling: ☺ ☺ ☺ ☹ ☹ ☹

	Due Date
Class #1 _____	_____
Class #2 _____	_____
Class #3 _____	_____
Class #4 _____	_____
Class #5 _____	_____
Class #6 _____	_____
Class #7 _____	_____

Meals	Water 8oz	Snacks	Water 8oz
1_____	☐	1_____	☐
2_____	☐	2_____	☐
3_____	☐	Responsibilities, Chores, Homework	☐

TUESDAY I'm feeling: ☺ ☺ ☺ ☹ ☹ ☹

	Due Date
Class #1 _____	_____
Class #2 _____	_____
Class #3 _____	_____
Class #4 _____	_____
Class #5 _____	_____
Class #6 _____	_____
Class #7 _____	_____

Meals	Water 8oz	Snacks	Water 8oz
1_____	☐	1_____	☐
2_____	☐	2_____	☐
3_____	☐	Responsibilities, Chores, Homework	☐

WEDNESDAY I'm feeling: ☺ ☺ ☺ ☹ ☹ ☹

	Due Date
Class #1 _____	_____
Class #2 _____	_____
Class #3 _____	_____
Class #4 _____	_____
Class #5 _____	_____
Class #6 _____	_____
Class #7 _____	_____

Meals	Water 8oz	Snacks	Water 8oz
1_____	☐	1_____	☐
2_____	☐	2_____	☐
3_____	☐	Responsibilities, Chores, Homework	☐

WEEK:_____/_____/20____

THURSDAY I'm feeling: 😊 😲 😟 😣 😖 😐

		Due Date
Class #1	_____	_____
Class #2	_____	_____
Class #3	_____	_____
Class #4	_____	_____
Class #5	_____	_____
Class #6	_____	_____
Class #7	_____	_____

Meals	Water 8oz	Snacks	Water 8oz
1_____	☐	1_____	☐
2_____	☐	2_____	☐
3_____	☐	Responsibilities, Chores, Homework	☐

FRIDAY I'm feeling: 😊 😲 😟 😣 😖 😐

		Due Date
Class #1	_____	_____
Class #2	_____	_____
Class #3	_____	_____
Class #4	_____	_____
Class #5	_____	_____
Class #6	_____	_____
Class #7	_____	_____

Meals	Water 8oz	Snacks	Water 8oz
1_____	☐	1_____	☐
2_____	☐	2_____	☐
3_____	☐	Responsibilities, Chores, Homework	☐

SATURDAY 😊 😲 😟 😣 😖 😐   **SUNDAY** 😊 😲 😟 😣 😖 😐

Responsibility, Chores, Homework ☐   Responsibility, Chores, Homework ☐

_____   _____
_____   _____
_____   _____
_____   _____

GOALS

Weekly _____

_____

Monthly _____

_____

WEEK: _____ / _____ /20_____

MONDAY I'm feeling: ☺ ☺ ☺ ☹ ☹ ☹

Due Date

Class #1 _____ _____
Class #2 _____ _____
Class #3 _____ _____
Class #4 _____ _____
Class #5 _____ _____
Class #6 _____ _____
Class #7 _____ _____

Meals   Water 8oz   Snacks   Water 8oz
1_____ ☐   1_____ ☐
2_____ ☐   2_____ ☐
3_____ ☐   Responsibilities, Chores, Homework ☐

TUESDAY I'm feeling: ☺ ☺ ☺ ☹ ☹ ☹

Due Date

Class #1 _____ _____
Class #2 _____ _____
Class #3 _____ _____
Class #4 _____ _____
Class #5 _____ _____
Class #6 _____ _____
Class #7 _____ _____

Meals   Water 8oz   Snacks   Water 8oz
1_____ ☐   1_____ ☐
2_____ ☐   2_____ ☐
3_____ ☐   Responsibilities, Chores, Homework ☐

WEDNESDAY I'm feeling: ☺ ☺ ☺ ☹ ☹ ☹

Due Date

Class #1 _____ _____
Class #2 _____ _____
Class #3 _____ _____
Class #4 _____ _____
Class #5 _____ _____
Class #6 _____ _____
Class #7 _____ _____

Meals   Water 8oz   Snacks   Water 8oz
1_____ ☐   1_____ ☐
2_____ ☐   2_____ ☐
3_____ ☐   Responsibilities, Chores, Homework ☐

WEEK:_____/_____/20_____

THURSDAY I'm feeling: ☺ ☺ ☺ ☹ 😩 😐

		Due Date
Class #1	_____	_____
Class #2	_____	_____
Class #3	_____	_____
Class #4	_____	_____
Class #5	_____	_____
Class #6	_____	_____
Class #7	_____	_____

Meals	Water 8oz	Snacks	Water 8oz
1_____	☐	1_____	☐
2_____	☐	2_____	☐
3_____	☐	Responsibilities, Chores, Homework	☐

FRIDAY I'm feeling: ☺ ☺ ☺ ☹ 😩 😐

		Due Date
Class #1	_____	_____
Class #2	_____	_____
Class #3	_____	_____
Class #4	_____	_____
Class #5	_____	_____
Class #6	_____	_____
Class #7	_____	_____

Meals	Water 8oz	Snacks	Water 8oz
1_____	☐	1_____	☐
2_____	☐	2_____	☐
3_____	☐	Responsibilities, Chores, Homework	☐

SATURDAY ☺ ☺ ☺ ☹ 😩 😐   SUNDAY ☺ ☺ ☺ ☹ 😩 😐

Responsibility, Chores, Homework ☐   Responsibility, Chores, Homework ☐

_____   _____
_____   _____
_____   _____
_____   _____

GOALS
Weekly _____
_____

Monthly _____
_____

WEEK: _____ / _____ /20_____

MONDAY   I'm feeling: ☺ 😐 😕 ☹ 😣 😫

		Due Date
Class #1	_____	_____
Class #2	_____	_____
Class #3	_____	_____
Class #4	_____	_____
Class #5	_____	_____
Class #6	_____	_____
Class #7	_____	_____

Meals   Water 8oz   Snacks   Water 8oz
1_____ ☐   1_____ ☐
2_____ ☐   2_____ ☐
3_____ ☐   Responsibilities, Chores, Homework ☐

TUESDAY   I'm feeling: ☺ 😐 😕 ☹ 😣 😫

		Due Date
Class #1	_____	_____
Class #2	_____	_____
Class #3	_____	_____
Class #4	_____	_____
Class #5	_____	_____
Class #6	_____	_____
Class #7	_____	_____

Meals   Water 8oz   Snacks   Water 8oz
1_____ ☐   1_____ ☐
2_____ ☐   2_____ ☐
3_____ ☐   Responsibilities, Chores, Homework ☐

WEDNESDAY I'm feeling: ☺ 😐 😕 ☹ 😣 😫

		Due Date
Class #1	_____	_____
Class #2	_____	_____
Class #3	_____	_____
Class #4	_____	_____
Class #5	_____	_____
Class #6	_____	_____
Class #7	_____	_____

Meals   Water 8oz   Snacks   Water 8oz
1_____ ☐   1_____ ☐
2_____ ☐   2_____ ☐
3_____ ☐   Responsibilities, Chores, Homework ☐

WEEK:_____/_____/20_____

THURSDAY I'm feeling: ☺ ☺ ☺ ☹ ☹ ☹

                                                 Due Date

Class #1 _____ _____
Class #2 _____ _____
Class #3 _____ _____
Class #4 _____ _____
Class #5 _____ _____
Class #6 _____ _____
Class #7 _____ _____

Meals   Water 8oz Snacks   Water 8oz
1_____ ☐ 1_____ ☐
2_____ ☐ 2_____ ☐
3_____ ☐ Responsibilities, Chores, Homework ☐

FRIDAY I'm feeling: ☺ ☺ ☺ ☹ ☹ ☹

                                                 Due Date

Class #1 _____ _____
Class #2 _____ _____
Class #3 _____ _____
Class #4 _____ _____
Class #5 _____ _____
Class #6 _____ _____
Class #7 _____ _____

Meals   Water 8oz Snacks   Water 8oz
1_____ ☐ 1_____ ☐
2_____ ☐ 2_____ ☐
3_____ ☐ Responsibilities, Chores, Homework ☐

SATURDAY ☺ ☺ ☺ ☹ ☹ ☹   **SUNDAY** ☺ ☺ ☺ ☹ ☹ ☹

Responsibility, Chores, Homework _____ ☐ Responsibility, Chores, Homework _____ ☐

_____ _____
_____ _____
_____ _____
_____ _____

GOALS
Weekly _____
             _____
Monthly _____
             _____

WEEK:_____/_____/20_____

MONDAY I'm feeling: ☺ 😐 😕 ☹ 😬 😵

		Due Date
Class #1	_____	_____
Class #2	_____	_____
Class #3	_____	_____
Class #4	_____	_____
Class #5	_____	_____
Class #6	_____	_____
Class #7	_____	_____

Meals	Water 8oz	Snacks	Water 8oz
1_____	☐	1_____	☐
2_____	☐	2_____	☐
3_____	☐	Responsibilities, Chores, Homework	☐

TUESDAY I'm feeling: ☺ 😐 😕 ☹ 😬 😵

		Due Date
Class #1	_____	_____
Class #2	_____	_____
Class #3	_____	_____
Class #4	_____	_____
Class #5	_____	_____
Class #6	_____	_____
Class #7	_____	_____

Meals	Water 8oz	Snacks	Water 8oz
1_____	☐	1_____	☐
2_____	☐	2_____	☐
3_____	☐	Responsibilities, Chores, Homework	☐

WEDNESDAY I'm feeling: ☺ 😐 😕 ☹ 😬 😵

		Due Date
Class #1	_____	_____
Class #2	_____	_____
Class #3	_____	_____
Class #4	_____	_____
Class #5	_____	_____
Class #6	_____	_____
Class #7	_____	_____

Meals	Water 8oz	Snacks	Water 8oz
1_____	☐	1_____	☐
2_____	☐	2_____	☐
3_____	☐	Responsibilities, Chores, Homework	☐

WEEK: _____ / _____ / 20 _____

THURSDAY I'm feeling: ☺ 😐 😕 ☹ 😣 😫

		Due Date
Class #1	_____	_____
Class #2	_____	_____
Class #3	_____	_____
Class #4	_____	_____
Class #5	_____	_____
Class #6	_____	_____
Class #7	_____	_____

Meals	Water 8oz	Snacks	Water 8oz
1_____	☐	1_____	☐
2_____	☐	2_____	☐
3_____	☐	Responsibilities, Chores, Homework	☐

FRIDAY I'm feeling: ☺ 😐 😕 ☹ 😣 😫

		Due Date
Class #1	_____	_____
Class #2	_____	_____
Class #3	_____	_____
Class #4	_____	_____
Class #5	_____	_____
Class #6	_____	_____
Class #7	_____	_____

Meals	Water 8oz	Snacks	Water 8oz
1_____	☐	1_____	☐
2_____	☐	2_____	☐
3_____	☐	Responsibilities, Chores, Homework	☐

SATURDAY ☺ 😐 😕 ☹ 😣 😫   **SUNDAY** ☺ 😐 😕 ☹ 😣 😫

Responsibility, Chores, Homework ☐	Responsibility, Chores, Homework ☐
_____	_____
_____	_____
_____	_____
_____	_____

GOALS

Weekly _____

Monthly _____

WEEK:_____/_____/20_____

MONDAY I'm feeling: ☺ ☹ 😕 ☹ 😣 😐

		Due Date
Class #1	_____	_____
Class #2	_____	_____
Class #3	_____	_____
Class #4	_____	_____
Class #5	_____	_____
Class #6	_____	_____
Class #7	_____	_____

Meals	Water 8oz	Snacks	Water 8oz
1_____	☐	1_____	☐
2_____	☐	2_____	☐
3_____	☐	Responsibilities, Chores, Homework	☐

TUESDAY I'm feeling: ☺ ☹ 😕 ☹ 😣 😐

		Due Date
Class #1	_____	_____
Class #2	_____	_____
Class #3	_____	_____
Class #4	_____	_____
Class #5	_____	_____
Class #6	_____	_____
Class #7	_____	_____

Meals	Water 8oz	Snacks	Water 8oz
1_____	☐	1_____	☐
2_____	☐	2_____	☐
3_____	☐	Responsibilities, Chores, Homework	☐

WEDNESDAY I'm feeling: ☺ ☹ 😕 ☹ 😣 😐

		Due Date
Class #1	_____	_____
Class #2	_____	_____
Class #3	_____	_____
Class #4	_____	_____
Class #5	_____	_____
Class #6	_____	_____
Class #7	_____	_____

Meals	Water 8oz	Snacks	Water 8oz
1_____	☐	1_____	☐
2_____	☐	2_____	☐
3_____	☐	Responsibilities, Chores, Homework	☐

WEEK:_____/_____/20_____

THURSDAY I'm feeling: ☺ ☺ ☺ ☹ ☹ ☹

		Due Date
Class #1	_____	_____
Class #2	_____	_____
Class #3	_____	_____
Class #4	_____	_____
Class #5	_____	_____
Class #6	_____	_____
Class #7	_____	_____

Meals   Water 8oz   Snacks   Water 8oz
1_____ ☐   1_____ ☐
2_____ ☐   2_____ ☐
3_____ ☐   Responsibilities, Chores, Homework ☐

FRIDAY I'm feeling: ☺ ☺ ☺ ☹ ☹ ☹

		Due Date
Class #1	_____	_____
Class #2	_____	_____
Class #3	_____	_____
Class #4	_____	_____
Class #5	_____	_____
Class #6	_____	_____
Class #7	_____	_____

Meals   Water 8oz   Snacks   Water 8oz
1_____ ☐   1_____ ☐
2_____ ☐   2_____ ☐
3_____ ☐   Responsibilities, Chores, Homework ☐

SATURDAY ☺ ☺ ☺ ☹ ☹ ☹   **SUNDAY** ☺ ☺ ☺ ☹ ☹ ☹

Responsibility, Chores, Homework _____ ☐   Responsibility, Chores, Homework ☐

_____   _____
_____   _____
_____   _____
_____   _____

GOALS

Weekly _____

_____

Monthly _____

_____

WEEK: _____/_____/20_____

MONDAY   I'm feeling: 😊 😮 😐 🙁 😬 😕

		Due Date
Class #1	_____	_____
Class #2	_____	_____
Class #3	_____	_____
Class #4	_____	_____
Class #5	_____	_____
Class #6	_____	_____
Class #7	_____	_____

Meals	Water 8oz	Snacks	Water 8oz
1_____	☐	1_____	☐
2_____	☐	2_____	☐
3_____	☐	Responsibilities, Chores, Homework	☐

TUESDAY   I'm feeling: 😊 😮 😐 🙁 😬 😕

		Due Date
Class #1	_____	_____
Class #2	_____	_____
Class #3	_____	_____
Class #4	_____	_____
Class #5	_____	_____
Class #6	_____	_____
Class #7	_____	_____

Meals	Water 8oz	Snacks	Water 8oz
1_____	☐	1_____	☐
2_____	☐	2_____	☐
3_____	☐	Responsibilities, Chores, Homework	☐

WEDNESDAY I'm feeling: 😊 😮 😐 🙁 😬 😕

		Due Date
Class #1	_____	_____
Class #2	_____	_____
Class #3	_____	_____
Class #4	_____	_____
Class #5	_____	_____
Class #6	_____	_____
Class #7	_____	_____

Meals	Water 8oz	Snacks	Water 8oz
1_____	☐	1_____	☐
2_____	☐	2_____	☐
3_____	☐	Responsibilities, Chores, Homework	☐

WEEK: _____/_____/20_____

THURSDAY I'm feeling: ☺ ☺ ☺ ☹ ☹ ☹

Due Date

Class #1 _____ _____
Class #2 _____ _____
Class #3 _____ _____
Class #4 _____ _____
Class #5 _____ _____
Class #6 _____ _____
Class #7 _____ _____

Meals	Water 8oz	Snacks	Water 8oz
1_____	☐	1_____	☐
2_____	☐	2_____	☐
3_____	☐	Responsibilities, Chores, Homework	☐

FRIDAY I'm feeling: ☺ ☺ ☺ ☹ ☹ ☹

Due Date

Class #1 _____ _____
Class #2 _____ _____
Class #3 _____ _____
Class #4 _____ _____
Class #5 _____ _____
Class #6 _____ _____
Class #7 _____ _____

Meals	Water 8oz	Snacks	Water 8oz
1_____	☐	1_____	☐
2_____	☐	2_____	☐
3_____	☐	Responsibilities, Chores, Homework	☐

SATURDAY ☺ ☺ ☺ ☹ ☹ ☹   **SUNDAY** ☺ ☺ ☺ ☹ ☹ ☹

Responsibility, Chores, Homework ☐   Responsibility, Chores, Homework ☐

_____   _____
_____   _____
_____   _____
_____   _____

GOALS

Weekly _____

Monthly _____

WEEK: _____ / _____ / 20 _____

MONDAY   I'm feeling: ☺ ☺ ☺ ☹ ☹ ☹

		Due Date
Class #1	_____	_____
Class #2	_____	_____
Class #3	_____	_____
Class #4	_____	_____
Class #5	_____	_____
Class #6	_____	_____
Class #7	_____	_____

Meals   Water 8oz   Snacks   Water 8oz

1_____ ☐   1_____ ☐

2_____ ☐   2_____ ☐

3_____ ☐   Responsibilities, Chores, Homework ☐

TUESDAY   I'm feeling: ☺ ☺ ☺ ☹ ☹ ☹

		Due Date
Class #1	_____	_____
Class #2	_____	_____
Class #3	_____	_____
Class #4	_____	_____
Class #5	_____	_____
Class #6	_____	_____
Class #7	_____	_____

Meals   Water 8oz   Snacks   Water 8oz

1_____ ☐   1_____ ☐

2_____ ☐   2_____ ☐

3_____ ☐   Responsibilities, Chores, Homework ☐

WEDNESDAY I'm feeling: ☺ ☺ ☺ ☹ ☹ ☹

		Due Date
Class #1	_____	_____
Class #2	_____	_____
Class #3	_____	_____
Class #4	_____	_____
Class #5	_____	_____
Class #6	_____	_____
Class #7	_____	_____

Meals   Water 8oz   Snacks   Water 8oz

1_____ ☐   1_____ ☐

2_____ ☐   2_____ ☐

3_____ ☐   Responsibilities, Chores, Homework ☐

WEEK:_____/_____/20____

THURSDAY I'm feeling: ☺ 😃 😕 ☹ 😖 😐

Due Date

Class #1 _____ _____

Class #2 _____ _____

Class #3 _____ _____

Class #4 _____ _____

Class #5 _____ _____

Class #6 _____ _____

Class #7 _____ _____

Meals	Water 8oz	Snacks	Water 8oz
1_____	☐	1_____	☐
2_____	☐	2_____	☐
3_____	☐	Responsibilities, Chores, Homework	☐

FRIDAY I'm feeling: ☺ 😃 😕 ☹ 😖 😐

Due Date

Class #1 _____ _____

Class #2 _____ _____

Class #3 _____ _____

Class #4 _____ _____

Class #5 _____ _____

Class #6 _____ _____

Class #7 _____ _____

Meals	Water 8oz	Snacks	Water 8oz
1_____	☐	1_____	☐
2_____	☐	2_____	☐
3_____	☐	Responsibilities, Chores, Homework	☐

SATURDAY ☺ 😃 😕 ☹ 😖 😐   SUNDAY ☺ 😃 😕 ☹ 😖 😐

Responsibility, Chores, Homework ☐   Responsibility, Chores, Homework ☐

_____   _____

_____   _____

_____   _____

_____   _____

GOALS

Weekly _____

_____

Monthly _____

_____

WEEK:_____/_____/20_____

MONDAY I'm feeling: ☺ ☺ ☺ ☹ 😬 😐

		Due Date
Class #1	_____	_____
Class #2	_____	_____
Class #3	_____	_____
Class #4	_____	_____
Class #5	_____	_____
Class #6	_____	_____
Class #7	_____	_____

Meals   Water 8oz   Snacks   Water 8oz
1_____ ☐   1_____ ☐
2_____ ☐   2_____ ☐
3_____ ☐   Responsibilities, Chores, Homework ☐

TUESDAY I'm feeling: ☺ ☺ ☺ ☹ 😬 😐

		Due Date
Class #1	_____	_____
Class #2	_____	_____
Class #3	_____	_____
Class #4	_____	_____
Class #5	_____	_____
Class #6	_____	_____
Class #7	_____	_____

Meals   Water 8oz   Snacks   Water 8oz
1_____ ☐   1_____ ☐
2_____ ☐   2_____ ☐
3_____ ☐   Responsibilities, Chores, Homework ☐

WEDNESDAY I'm feeling: ☺ ☺ ☺ ☹ 😬 😐

		Due Date
Class #1	_____	_____
Class #2	_____	_____
Class #3	_____	_____
Class #4	_____	_____
Class #5	_____	_____
Class #6	_____	_____
Class #7	_____	_____

Meals   Water 8oz   Snacks   Water 8oz
1_____ ☐   1_____ ☐
2_____ ☐   2_____ ☐
3_____ ☐   Responsibilities, Chores, Homework ☐

WEEK:_____/_____/20____

THURSDAY   I'm feeling: ☺ ☺ ☺ ☹ ☹ ☹

		Due Date
Class #1	_____	_____
Class #2	_____	_____
Class #3	_____	_____
Class #4	_____	_____
Class #5	_____	_____
Class #6	_____	_____
Class #7	_____	_____

Meals	Water 8oz	Snacks	Water 8oz
1_____	☐	1_____	☐
2_____	☐	2_____	☐
3_____	☐	Responsibilities, Chores, Homework	☐

FRIDAY   I'm feeling: ☺ ☺ ☺ ☹ ☹ ☹

		Due Date
Class #1	_____	_____
Class #2	_____	_____
Class #3	_____	_____
Class #4	_____	_____
Class #5	_____	_____
Class #6	_____	_____
Class #7	_____	_____

Meals	Water 8oz	Snacks	Water 8oz
1_____	☐	1_____	☐
2_____	☐	2_____	☐
3_____	☐	Responsibilities, Chores, Homework	☐

SATURDAY ☺ ☺ ☺ ☹ ☹ ☹   SUNDAY ☺ ☺ ☺ ☹ ☹ ☹

Responsibility, Chores, Homework ☐	Responsibility, Chores, Homework ☐
_____	_____
_____	_____
_____	_____
_____	_____

GOALS
Weekly _____

Monthly _____

WEEK: _____ / _____ /20_____

MONDAY I'm feeling: 😊 😟 😖 😣 😩 😐

		Due Date
Class #1	_____	_____
Class #2	_____	_____
Class #3	_____	_____
Class #4	_____	_____
Class #5	_____	_____
Class #6	_____	_____
Class #7	_____	_____

Meals   Water 8oz   Snacks   Water 8oz
1_____   ☐   1_____   ☐
2_____   ☐   2_____   ☐
3_____   ☐   Responsibilities, Chores, Homework ☐

TUESDAY I'm feeling: 😊 😟 😖 😣 😩 😐

		Due Date
Class #1	_____	_____
Class #2	_____	_____
Class #3	_____	_____
Class #4	_____	_____
Class #5	_____	_____
Class #6	_____	_____
Class #7	_____	_____

Meals   Water 8oz   Snacks   Water 8oz
1_____   ☐   1_____   ☐
2_____   ☐   2_____   ☐
3_____   ☐   Responsibilities, Chores, Homework ☐

WEDNESDAY I'm feeling: 😊 😟 😖 😣 😩 😐

		Due Date
Class #1	_____	_____
Class #2	_____	_____
Class #3	_____	_____
Class #4	_____	_____
Class #5	_____	_____
Class #6	_____	_____
Class #7	_____	_____

Meals   Water 8oz   Snacks   Water 8oz
1_____   ☐   1_____   ☐
2_____   ☐   2_____   ☐
3_____   ☐   Responsibilities, Chores, Homework ☐

WEEK:_____/_____/20_____

THURSDAY I'm feeling: ☺ 😐 😕 ☹ 😫 😬

Due Date

Class #1 _____ _____
Class #2 _____ _____
Class #3 _____ _____
Class #4 _____ _____
Class #5 _____ _____
Class #6 _____ _____
Class #7 _____ _____

Meals   Water 8oz   Snacks   Water 8oz
1_____ ☐ 1_____ ☐
2_____ ☐ 2_____ ☐
3_____ ☐ Responsibilities, Chores, Homework ☐

FRIDAY I'm feeling: ☺ 😐 😕 ☹ 😫 😬

Due Date

Class #1 _____ _____
Class #2 _____ _____
Class #3 _____ _____
Class #4 _____ _____
Class #5 _____ _____
Class #6 _____ _____
Class #7 _____ _____

Meals   Water 8oz   Snacks   Water 8oz
1_____ ☐ 1_____ ☐
2_____ ☐ 2_____ ☐
3_____ ☐ Responsibilities, Chores, Homework ☐

SATURDAY ☺ 😐 😕 ☹ 😫 😬   ## SUNDAY ☺ 😐 😕 ☹ 😫 😬

Responsibility, Chores, Homework ☐   Responsibility, Chores, Homework ☐
_____   _____
_____   _____
_____   _____
_____   _____

GOALS
Weekly   _____
         _____
Monthly _____
         _____

<table>
<tr><td colspan="2">WEEK: _____ / _____ /20_____</td></tr>
</table>

MONDAY I'm feeling: 😊 😮 😕 😟 😬 😣

		Due Date
Class #1	_____	_____
Class #2	_____	_____
Class #3	_____	_____
Class #4	_____	_____
Class #5	_____	_____
Class #6	_____	_____
Class #7	_____	_____

Meals	Water 8oz	Snacks	Water 8oz
1_____	☐	1_____	☐
2_____	☐	2_____	☐
3_____	☐	Responsibilities, Chores, Homework	☐

TUESDAY I'm feeling: 😊 😮 😕 😟 😬 😣

		Due Date
Class #1	_____	_____
Class #2	_____	_____
Class #3	_____	_____
Class #4	_____	_____
Class #5	_____	_____
Class #6	_____	_____
Class #7	_____	_____

Meals	Water 8oz	Snacks	Water 8oz
1_____	☐	1_____	☐
2_____	☐	2_____	☐
3_____	☐	Responsibilities, Chores, Homework	☐

WEDNESDAY I'm feeling: 😊 😮 😕 😟 😬 😣

		Due Date
Class #1	_____	_____
Class #2	_____	_____
Class #3	_____	_____
Class #4	_____	_____
Class #5	_____	_____
Class #6	_____	_____
Class #7	_____	_____

Meals	Water 8oz	Snacks	Water 8oz
1_____	☐	1_____	☐
2_____	☐	2_____	☐
3_____	☐	Responsibilities, Chores, Homework	☐

WEEK:_____/_____/20_____

THURSDAY I'm feeling: ☺ 😐 😕 ☹ 😫 😐

		Due Date
Class #1	_____	_____
Class #2	_____	_____
Class #3	_____	_____
Class #4	_____	_____
Class #5	_____	_____
Class #6	_____	_____
Class #7	_____	_____

Meals	Water 8oz	Snacks	Water 8oz
1_____	☐	1_____	☐
2_____	☐	2_____	☐
3_____	☐	Responsibilities, Chores, Homework	☐

FRIDAY I'm feeling: ☺ 😐 😕 ☹ 😫 😐

		Due Date
Class #1	_____	_____
Class #2	_____	_____
Class #3	_____	_____
Class #4	_____	_____
Class #5	_____	_____
Class #6	_____	_____
Class #7	_____	_____

Meals	Water 8oz	Snacks	Water 8oz
1_____	☐	1_____	☐
2_____	☐	2_____	☐
3_____	☐	Responsibilities, Chores, Homework	☐

SATURDAY ☺ 😐 😕 ☹ 😫 😐   **SUNDAY** ☺ 😐 😕 ☹ 😫 😐

Responsibility, Chores, Homework ☐	Responsibility, Chores, Homework ☐
_____	_____
_____	_____
_____	_____
_____	_____

GOALS

Weekly _____

_____

Monthly _____

_____

WEEK:_____/_____/20_____

MONDAY I'm feeling: 🙂 😬 😐 🙁 😖 😕

		Due Date
Class #1	_____	_____
Class #2	_____	_____
Class #3	_____	_____
Class #4	_____	_____
Class #5	_____	_____
Class #6	_____	_____
Class #7	_____	_____

Meals	Water 8oz	Snacks	Water 8oz
1_____	☐	1_____	☐
2_____	☐	2_____	☐
3_____	☐	Responsibilities, Chores, Homework	☐

TUESDAY I'm feeling: 🙂 😬 😐 🙁 😖 😕

		Due Date
Class #1	_____	_____
Class #2	_____	_____
Class #3	_____	_____
Class #4	_____	_____
Class #5	_____	_____
Class #6	_____	_____
Class #7	_____	_____

Meals	Water 8oz	Snacks	Water 8oz
1_____	☐	1_____	☐
2_____	☐	2_____	☐
3_____	☐	Responsibilities, Chores, Homework	☐

WEDNESDAY I'm feeling: 🙂 😬 😐 🙁 😖 😕

		Due Date
Class #1	_____	_____
Class #2	_____	_____
Class #3	_____	_____
Class #4	_____	_____
Class #5	_____	_____
Class #6	_____	_____
Class #7	_____	_____

Meals	Water 8oz	Snacks	Water 8oz
1_____	☐	1_____	☐
2_____	☐	2_____	☐
3_____	☐	Responsibilities, Chores, Homework	☐

WEEK:_____/_____/20_____

THURSDAY I'm feeling: ☺ 😐 😕 😣 😫 😬

Due Date

Class #1 _____ _____

Class #2 _____ _____

Class #3 _____ _____

Class #4 _____ _____

Class #5 _____ _____

Class #6 _____ _____

Class #7 _____ _____

Meals	Water 8oz	Snacks	Water 8oz
1_____	☐	1_____	☐
2_____	☐	2_____	☐
3_____	☐	Responsibilities, Chores, Homework	☐

FRIDAY I'm feeling: ☺ 😐 😕 😣 😫 😬

Due Date

Class #1 _____ _____

Class #2 _____ _____

Class #3 _____ _____

Class #4 _____ _____

Class #5 _____ _____

Class #6 _____ _____

Class #7 _____ _____

Meals	Water 8oz	Snacks	Water 8oz
1_____	☐	1_____	☐
2_____	☐	2_____	☐
3_____	☐	Responsibilities, Chores, Homework	☐

SATURDAY ☺ 😐 😕 😣 😫 😬   **SUNDAY** ☺ 😐 😕 😣 😫 😬

Responsibility, Chores, Homework ☐   Responsibility, Chores, Homework ☐

_____   _____

_____   _____

_____   _____

_____   _____

GOALS

Weekly _____

_____

Monthly _____

_____

WEEK: _____ / _____ /20_____

MONDAY   I'm feeling: ☺ 😐 🙁 😧 😫 😑

			Due Date
Class #1 _____			_____
Class #2 _____			_____
Class #3 _____			_____
Class #4 _____			_____
Class #5 _____			_____
Class #6 _____			_____
Class #7 _____			_____

Meals	Water 8oz	Snacks	Water 8oz
1_____	☐	1_____	☐
2_____	☐	2_____	☐
3_____	☐	Responsibilities, Chores, Homework	☐

TUESDAY   I'm feeling: ☺ 😐 🙁 😧 😫 😑

			Due Date
Class #1 _____			_____
Class #2 _____			_____
Class #3 _____			_____
Class #4 _____			_____
Class #5 _____			_____
Class #6 _____			_____
Class #7 _____			_____

Meals	Water 8oz	Snacks	Water 8oz
1_____	☐	1_____	☐
2_____	☐	2_____	☐
3_____	☐	Responsibilities, Chores, Homework	☐

WEDNESDAY   I'm feeling: ☺ 😐 🙁 😧 😫 😑

			Due Date
Class #1 _____			_____
Class #2 _____			_____
Class #3 _____			_____
Class #4 _____			_____
Class #5 _____			_____
Class #6 _____			_____
Class #7 _____			_____

Meals	Water 8oz	Snacks	Water 8oz
1_____	☐	1_____	☐
2_____	☐	2_____	☐
3_____	☐	Responsibilities, Chores, Homework	☐

WEEK: _____ / _____ /20 _____

THURSDAY I'm feeling: ☺ 😐 😕 ☹ 😫 😑

		Due Date
Class #1	_____	_____
Class #2	_____	_____
Class #3	_____	_____
Class #4	_____	_____
Class #5	_____	_____
Class #6	_____	_____
Class #7	_____	_____

Meals   Water 8oz   Snacks   Water 8oz
1_____ ☐   1_____ ☐
2_____ ☐   2_____ ☐
3_____ ☐   Responsibilities, Chores, Homework ☐

FRIDAY I'm feeling: ☺ 😐 😕 ☹ 😫 😑

		Due Date
Class #1	_____	_____
Class #2	_____	_____
Class #3	_____	_____
Class #4	_____	_____
Class #5	_____	_____
Class #6	_____	_____
Class #7	_____	_____

Meals   Water 8oz   Snacks   Water 8oz
1_____ ☐   1_____ ☐
2_____ ☐   2_____ ☐
3_____ ☐   Responsibilities, Chores, Homework ☐

SATURDAY ☺ 😐 😕 ☹ 😫 😑   **SUNDAY** ☺ 😐 😕 ☹ 😫 😑

Responsibility, Chores, Homework ☐   Responsibility, Chores, Homework ☐

_____   _____
_____   _____
_____   _____
_____   _____

GOALS
Weekly _____
_____
Monthly _____
_____

WEEK:_____/_____/20_____

MONDAY   I'm feeling: ☺ 😐 😕 ☹ 😣 😑

		Due Date
Class #1	_____	_____
Class #2	_____	_____
Class #3	_____	_____
Class #4	_____	_____
Class #5	_____	_____
Class #6	_____	_____
Class #7	_____	

Meals	Water 8oz	Snacks	Water 8oz
1_____	☐	1_____	☐
2_____	☐	2_____	☐
3_____	☐	Responsibilities, Chores, Homework	☐

TUESDAY   I'm feeling: ☺ 😐 😕 ☹ 😣 😑

		Due Date
Class #1	_____	_____
Class #2	_____	_____
Class #3	_____	_____
Class #4	_____	_____
Class #5	_____	_____
Class #6	_____	_____
Class #7	_____	

Meals	Water 8oz	Snacks	Water 8oz
1_____	☐	1_____	☐
2_____	☐	2_____	☐
3_____	☐	Responsibilities, Chores, Homework	☐

WEDNESDAY I'm feeling: ☺ 😐 😕 ☹ 😣 😑

		Due Date
Class #1	_____	_____
Class #2	_____	_____
Class #3	_____	_____
Class #4	_____	_____
Class #5	_____	_____
Class #6	_____	_____
Class #7	_____	

Meals	Water 8oz	Snacks	Water 8oz
1_____	☐	1_____	☐
2_____	☐	2_____	☐
3_____	☐	Responsibilities, Chores, Homework	☐

WEEK: _____ / _____ /20____

THURSDAY I'm feeling: ☺ 😐 😕 ☹ 😫 😤

Due Date

Class #1 _____ _____

Class #2 _____ _____

Class #3 _____ _____

Class #4 _____ _____

Class #5 _____ _____

Class #6 _____ _____

Class #7 _____ _____

Meals	Water 8oz	Snacks	Water 8oz
1_____	☐	1_____	☐
2_____	☐	2_____	☐
3_____	☐	Responsibilities, Chores, Homework	☐

FRIDAY I'm feeling: ☺ 😐 😕 ☹ 😫 😤

Due Date

Class #1 _____ _____

Class #2 _____ _____

Class #3 _____ _____

Class #4 _____ _____

Class #5 _____ _____

Class #6 _____ _____

Class #7 _____ _____

Meals	Water 8oz	Snacks	Water 8oz
1_____	☐	1_____	☐
2_____	☐	2_____	☐
3_____	☐	Responsibilities, Chores, Homework	☐

SATURDAY ☺ 😐 😕 ☹ 😫 😤   **SUNDAY** ☺ 😐 😕 ☹ 😫 😤

Responsibility, Chores, Homework _____ ☐   Responsibility, Chores, Homework _____ ☐

_____   _____

_____   _____

_____   _____

_____   _____

GOALS

Weekly _____

_____

Monthly _____

_____

WEEK:_____/_____/20_____

MONDAY I'm feeling: ☺ 😬 😕 😟 😣 😐

		Due Date
Class #1	_____	_____
Class #2	_____	_____
Class #3	_____	_____
Class #4	_____	_____
Class #5	_____	_____
Class #6	_____	_____
Class #7	_____	

Meals	Water 8oz	Snacks	Water 8oz
1_____	☐	1_____	☐
2_____	☐	2_____	☐
3_____	☐	Responsibilities, Chores, Homework	☐

TUESDAY I'm feeling: ☺ 😬 😕 😟 😣 😐

		Due Date
Class #1	_____	_____
Class #2	_____	_____
Class #3	_____	_____
Class #4	_____	_____
Class #5	_____	_____
Class #6	_____	_____
Class #7	_____	

Meals	Water 8oz	Snacks	Water 8oz
1_____	☐	1_____	☐
2_____	☐	2_____	☐
3_____	☐	Responsibilities, Chores, Homework	☐

WEDNESDAY I'm feeling: ☺ 😬 😕 😟 😣 😐

		Due Date
Class #1	_____	_____
Class #2	_____	_____
Class #3	_____	_____
Class #4	_____	_____
Class #5	_____	_____
Class #6	_____	_____
Class #7	_____	

Meals	Water 8oz	Snacks	Water 8oz
1_____	☐	1_____	☐
2_____	☐	2_____	☐
3_____	☐	Responsibilities, Chores, Homework	☐

WEEK:_____/ _____/20____

THURSDAY   I'm feeling: ☺ 😮 😕 ☹ 😣 😐

Due Date

Class #1 _____   _____
Class #2 _____   _____
Class #3 _____   _____
Class #4 _____   _____
Class #5 _____   _____
Class #6 _____   _____
Class #7 _____   _____

Meals   Water 8oz   Snacks   Water 8oz
1_____ ☐   1_____ ☐
2_____ ☐   2_____ ☐
3_____ ☐   Responsibilities, Chores, Homework ☐

FRIDAY   I'm feeling: ☺ 😮 😕 ☹ 😣 😐

Due Date

Class #1 _____   _____
Class #2 _____   _____
Class #3 _____   _____
Class #4 _____   _____
Class #5 _____   _____
Class #6 _____   _____
Class #7 _____   _____

Meals   Water 8oz   Snacks   Water 8oz
1_____ ☐   1_____ ☐
2_____ ☐   2_____ ☐
3_____ ☐   Responsibilities, Chores, Homework ☐

SATURDAY ☺ 😮 😕 ☹ 😣 😐   ## SUNDAY ☺ 😮 😕 ☹ 😣 😐

Responsibility, Chores, Homework _____ ☐   Responsibility, Chores, Homework _____ ☐

_____   _____
_____   _____
_____   _____
_____   _____

GOALS
Weekly _____
        _____
Monthly _____
        _____

WEEK: _____ / _____ /20_____

MONDAY I'm feeling: ☺ 😐 😕 ☹ 😣 😶

		Due Date
Class #1	_____	_____
Class #2	_____	_____
Class #3	_____	_____
Class #4	_____	_____
Class #5	_____	_____
Class #6	_____	_____
Class #7	_____	_____

Meals   Water 8oz   Snacks   Water 8oz
1_____ ☐ 1_____ ☐
2_____ ☐ 2_____ ☐
3_____ ☐ Responsibilities, Chores, Homework ☐

TUESDAY I'm feeling: ☺ 😐 😕 ☹ 😣 😶

		Due Date
Class #1	_____	_____
Class #2	_____	_____
Class #3	_____	_____
Class #4	_____	_____
Class #5	_____	_____
Class #6	_____	_____
Class #7	_____	_____

Meals   Water 8oz   Snacks   Water 8oz
1_____ ☐ 1_____ ☐
2_____ ☐ 2_____ ☐
3_____ ☐ Responsibilities, Chores, Homework ☐

WEDNESDAY I'm feeling: ☺ 😐 😕 ☹ 😣 😶

		Due Date
Class #1	_____	_____
Class #2	_____	_____
Class #3	_____	_____
Class #4	_____	_____
Class #5	_____	_____
Class #6	_____	_____
Class #7	_____	_____

Meals   Water 8oz   Snacks   Water 8oz
1_____ ☐ 1_____ ☐
2_____ ☐ 2_____ ☐
3_____ ☐ Responsibilities, Chores, Homework ☐

WEEK: _____ / _____ /20_____

THURSDAY I'm feeling: ☺ 😐 😕 ☹ 😫 😤

Due Date

Class #1 _____ _____

Class #2 _____ _____

Class #3 _____ _____

Class #4 _____ _____

Class #5 _____ _____

Class #6 _____ _____

Class #7 _____ _____

Meals   Water 8oz   Snacks   Water 8oz

1_____ ☐ 1_____ ☐

2_____ ☐ 2_____ ☐

3_____ ☐ Responsibilities, Chores, Homework ☐

FRIDAY I'm feeling: ☺ 😐 😕 ☹ 😫 😤

Due Date

Class #1 _____ _____

Class #2 _____ _____

Class #3 _____ _____

Class #4 _____ _____

Class #5 _____ _____

Class #6 _____ _____

Class #7 _____ _____

Meals   Water 8oz   Snacks   Water 8oz

1_____ ☐ 1_____ ☐

2_____ ☐ 2_____ ☐

3_____ ☐ Responsibilities, Chores, Homework ☐

SATURDAY ☺ 😐 😕 ☹ 😫 😤   **SUNDAY** ☺ 😐 😕 ☹ 😫 😤

Responsibility, Chores, Homework ☐   Responsibility, Chores, Homework ☐

_____   _____

_____   _____

_____   _____

_____   _____

GOALS

Weekly _____

_____

Monthly _____

_____

WEEK:_____/_____/20_____

MONDAY I'm feeling: ☺ 😲 😕 ☹ 😣 😐

		Due Date
Class #1	_____	_____
Class #2	_____	_____
Class #3	_____	_____
Class #4	_____	_____
Class #5	_____	_____
Class #6	_____	_____
Class #7	_____	_____

Meals	Water 8oz	Snacks	Water 8oz
1_____	☐	1_____	☐
2_____	☐	2_____	☐
3_____	☐	Responsibilities, Chores, Homework	☐

TUESDAY I'm feeling: ☺ 😲 😕 ☹ 😣 😐

		Due Date
Class #1	_____	_____
Class #2	_____	_____
Class #3	_____	_____
Class #4	_____	_____
Class #5	_____	_____
Class #6	_____	_____
Class #7	_____	_____

Meals	Water 8oz	Snacks	Water 8oz
1_____	☐	1_____	☐
2_____	☐	2_____	☐
3_____	☐	Responsibilities, Chores, Homework	☐

WEDNESDAY I'm feeling: ☺ 😲 😕 ☹ 😣 😐

		Due Date
Class #1	_____	_____
Class #2	_____	_____
Class #3	_____	_____
Class #4	_____	_____
Class #5	_____	_____
Class #6	_____	_____
Class #7	_____	_____

Meals	Water 8oz	Snacks	Water 8oz
1_____	☐	1_____	☐
2_____	☐	2_____	☐
3_____	☐	Responsibilities, Chores, Homework	☐

WEEK:_____/_____/20_____

THURSDAY I'm feeling: ☺ 😐 😕 ☹ 😣 😶

	Due Date
Class #1 _____	_____
Class #2 _____	_____
Class #3 _____	_____
Class #4 _____	_____
Class #5 _____	_____
Class #6 _____	_____
Class #7 _____	

Meals	Water 8oz	Snacks	Water 8oz
1_____	☐	1_____	☐
2_____	☐	2_____	☐
3_____	☐	Responsibilities, Chores, Homework	☐

FRIDAY I'm feeling: ☺ 😐 😕 ☹ 😣 😶

	Due Date
Class #1 _____	_____
Class #2 _____	_____
Class #3 _____	_____
Class #4 _____	_____
Class #5 _____	_____
Class #6 _____	_____
Class #7 _____	

Meals	Water 8oz	Snacks	Water 8oz
1_____	☐	1_____	☐
2_____	☐	2_____	☐
3_____	☐	Responsibilities, Chores, Homework	☐

SATURDAY ☺ 😐 😕 ☹ 😣 😶   SUNDAY ☺ 😐 😕 ☹ 😣 😶

Responsibility, Chores, Homework ☐	Responsibility, Chores, Homework ☐
_____	_____
_____	_____
_____	_____
_____	_____

GOALS
Weekly _____

Monthly _____

WEEK: _____ / _____ /20 _____

MONDAY I'm feeling: 😊 😣 😜 😦 😫 😐

Due Date

Class #1 _____ _____
Class #2 _____ _____
Class #3 _____ _____
Class #4 _____ _____
Class #5 _____ _____
Class #6 _____ _____
Class #7 _____ _____

Meals   Water 8oz   Snacks   Water 8oz

1_____ ☐ 1_____ ☐
2_____ ☐ 2_____ ☐
3_____ ☐ Responsibilities, Chores, Homework ☐

TUESDAY I'm feeling: 😊 😣 😜 😦 😫 😐

Due Date

Class #1 _____ _____
Class #2 _____ _____
Class #3 _____ _____
Class #4 _____ _____
Class #5 _____ _____
Class #6 _____ _____
Class #7 _____ _____

Meals   Water 8oz   Snacks   Water 8oz

1_____ ☐ 1_____ ☐
2_____ ☐ 2_____ ☐
3_____ ☐ Responsibilities, Chores, Homework ☐

WEDNESDAY I'm feeling: 😊 😣 😜 😦 😫 😐

Due Date

Class #1 _____ _____
Class #2 _____ _____
Class #3 _____ _____
Class #4 _____ _____
Class #5 _____ _____
Class #6 _____ _____
Class #7 _____ _____

Meals   Water 8oz   Snacks   Water 8oz

1_____ ☐ 1_____ ☐
2_____ ☐ 2_____ ☐
3_____ ☐ Responsibilities, Chores, Homework ☐

WEEK:_____/ _____/20_____

THURSDAY   I'm feeling: 😊 😦 😕 🙁 😣 😐

	Due Date
Class #1 _____	_____
Class #2 _____	_____
Class #3 _____	_____
Class #4 _____	_____
Class #5 _____	_____
Class #6 _____	_____
Class #7 _____	_____

Meals   Water 8oz   Snacks   Water 8oz
1_____ ☐   1_____ ☐
2_____ ☐   2_____ ☐
3_____ ☐   Responsibilities, Chores, Homework ☐

FRIDAY   I'm feeling: 😊 😦 😕 🙁 😣 😐

	Due Date
Class #1 _____	_____
Class #2 _____	_____
Class #3 _____	_____
Class #4 _____	_____
Class #5 _____	_____
Class #6 _____	_____
Class #7 _____	_____

Meals   Water 8oz   Snacks   Water 8oz
1_____ ☐   1_____ ☐
2_____ ☐   2_____ ☐
3_____ ☐   Responsibilities, Chores, Homework ☐

SATURDAY 😊 😦 😕 🙁 😣 😐   SUNDAY 😊 😦 😕 🙁 😣 😐

Responsibility, Chores, Homework ☐   Responsibility, Chores, Homework ☐

_____   _____
_____   _____
_____   _____
_____   _____

GOALS
Weekly _____
        _____
Monthly _____
        _____

WEEK:_____/_____/20_____

MONDAY   I'm feeling: ☺ 😐 😕 ☹ 😖 😑

	Due Date
Class #1 _____	_____
Class #2 _____	_____
Class #3 _____	_____
Class #4 _____	_____
Class #5 _____	_____
Class #6 _____	_____
Class #7 _____	_____

Meals	Water 8oz	Snacks	Water 8oz
1_____	☐	1_____	☐
2_____	☐	2_____	☐
3_____	☐	Responsibilities, Chores, Homework	☐

TUESDAY   I'm feeling: ☺ 😐 😕 ☹ 😖 😑

	Due Date
Class #1 _____	_____
Class #2 _____	_____
Class #3 _____	_____
Class #4 _____	_____
Class #5 _____	_____
Class #6 _____	_____
Class #7 _____	_____

Meals	Water 8oz	Snacks	Water 8oz
1_____	☐	1_____	☐
2_____	☐	2_____	☐
3_____	☐	Responsibilities, Chores, Homework	☐

WEDNESDAY   I'm feeling: ☺ 😐 😕 ☹ 😖 😑

	Due Date
Class #1 _____	_____
Class #2 _____	_____
Class #3 _____	_____
Class #4 _____	_____
Class #5 _____	_____
Class #6 _____	_____
Class #7 _____	_____

Meals	Water 8oz	Snacks	Water 8oz
1_____	☐	1_____	☐
2_____	☐	2_____	☐
3_____	☐	Responsibilities, Chores, Homework	☐

WEEK:_____/_____/20____

THURSDAY I'm feeling: 🙂 😐 😕 ☹️ 😫 😑

		Due Date
Class #1 _____		_____
Class #2 _____		_____
Class #3 _____		_____
Class #4 _____		_____
Class #5 _____		_____
Class #6 _____		_____
Class #7 _____		_____

Meals	Water 8oz	Snacks	Water 8oz
1_____	☐	1_____	☐
2_____	☐	2_____	☐
3_____	☐	Responsibilities, Chores, Homework	☐

FRIDAY I'm feeling: 🙂 😐 😕 ☹️ 😫 😑

		Due Date
Class #1 _____		_____
Class #2 _____		_____
Class #3 _____		_____
Class #4 _____		_____
Class #5 _____		_____
Class #6 _____		_____
Class #7 _____		_____

Meals	Water 8oz	Snacks	Water 8oz
1_____	☐	1_____	☐
2_____	☐	2_____	☐
3_____	☐	Responsibilities, Chores, Homework	☐

SATURDAY 🙂 😐 😕 ☹️ 😫 😑   SUNDAY 🙂 😐 😕 ☹️ 😫 😑

Responsibility, Chores, Homework ☐	Responsibility, Chores, Homework ☐
_____	_____
_____	_____
_____	_____
_____	_____

GOALS
Weekly _____

Monthly _____

WEEK: _____ / _____ /20_____

MONDAY   I'm feeling: ☺ ☺ ☺ ☹ 😖 😐

		Due Date
Class #1	_____	_____
Class #2	_____	_____
Class #3	_____	_____
Class #4	_____	_____
Class #5	_____	_____
Class #6	_____	_____
Class #7	_____	_____

Meals	Water 8oz	Snacks	Water 8oz
1_____	☐	1_____	☐
2_____	☐	2_____	☐
3_____	☐	Responsibilities, Chores, Homework	☐

TUESDAY   I'm feeling: ☺ ☺ ☺ ☹ 😖 😐

		Due Date
Class #1	_____	_____
Class #2	_____	_____
Class #3	_____	_____
Class #4	_____	_____
Class #5	_____	_____
Class #6	_____	_____
Class #7	_____	_____

Meals	Water 8oz	Snacks	Water 8oz
1_____	☐	1_____	☐
2_____	☐	2_____	☐
3_____	☐	Responsibilities, Chores, Homework	☐

WEDNESDAY I'm feeling: ☺ ☺ ☺ ☹ 😖 😐

		Due Date
Class #1	_____	_____
Class #2	_____	_____
Class #3	_____	_____
Class #4	_____	_____
Class #5	_____	_____
Class #6	_____	_____
Class #7	_____	_____

Meals	Water 8oz	Snacks	Water 8oz
1_____	☐	1_____	☐
2_____	☐	2_____	☐
3_____	☐	Responsibilities, Chores, Homework	☐

WEEK:_____/_____/20_____

THURSDAY   I'm feeling: 😊 😲 😜 😣 😫 😐

		Due Date
Class #1	_____	_____
Class #2	_____	_____
Class #3	_____	_____
Class #4	_____	_____
Class #5	_____	_____
Class #6	_____	_____
Class #7	_____	_____

Meals	Water 8oz	Snacks	Water 8oz
1_____	☐	1_____	☐
2_____	☐	2_____	☐
3_____	☐	Responsibilities, Chores, Homework	☐

FRIDAY   I'm feeling: 😊 😲 😜 😣 😫 😐

		Due Date
Class #1	_____	_____
Class #2	_____	_____
Class #3	_____	_____
Class #4	_____	_____
Class #5	_____	_____
Class #6	_____	_____
Class #7	_____	_____

Meals	Water 8oz	Snacks	Water 8oz
1_____	☐	1_____	☐
2_____	☐	2_____	☐
3_____	☐	Responsibilities, Chores, Homework	☐

SATURDAY 😊 😲 😜 😣 😫 😐   SUNDAY 😊 😲 😜 😣 😫 😐

Responsibility, Chores, Homework ☐	Responsibility, Chores, Homework ☐
_____	_____
_____	_____
_____	_____
_____	_____

GOALS
Weekly _____

_____

Monthly _____

_____

WEEK:_____/_____/20_____

MONDAY   I'm feeling: 😊 😟 😵 😣 😫 😐

		Due Date
Class #1	_____	_____
Class #2	_____	_____
Class #3	_____	_____
Class #4	_____	_____
Class #5	_____	_____
Class #6	_____	_____
Class #7	_____	_____

Meals	Water 8oz	Snacks	Water 8oz
1_____	☐	1_____	☐
2_____	☐	2_____	☐
3_____	☐	Responsibilities, Chores, Homework	☐

TUESDAY   I'm feeling: 😊 😟 😵 😣 😫 😐

		Due Date
Class #1	_____	_____
Class #2	_____	_____
Class #3	_____	_____
Class #4	_____	_____
Class #5	_____	_____
Class #6	_____	_____
Class #7	_____	_____

Meals	Water 8oz	Snacks	Water 8oz
1_____	☐	1_____	☐
2_____	☐	2_____	☐
3_____	☐	Responsibilities, Chores, Homework	☐

WEDNESDAY I'm feeling: 😊 😟 😵 😣 😫 😐

		Due Date
Class #1	_____	_____
Class #2	_____	_____
Class #3	_____	_____
Class #4	_____	_____
Class #5	_____	_____
Class #6	_____	_____
Class #7	_____	_____

Meals	Water 8oz	Snacks	Water 8oz
1_____	☐	1_____	☐
2_____	☐	2_____	☐
3_____	☐	Responsibilities, Chores, Homework	☐

WEEK:_____/_____/20____

THURSDAY I'm feeling: ☺ 😲 😕 ☹ 😫 😐

		Due Date
Class #1	_____	_____
Class #2	_____	_____
Class #3	_____	_____
Class #4	_____	_____
Class #5	_____	_____
Class #6	_____	_____
Class #7	_____	_____

Meals   Water 8oz   Snacks   Water 8oz
1_____ ☐   1_____ ☐
2_____ ☐   2_____ ☐
3_____ ☐   Responsibilities, Chores, Homework ☐

FRIDAY I'm feeling: ☺ 😲 😕 ☹ 😫 😐

		Due Date
Class #1	_____	_____
Class #2	_____	_____
Class #3	_____	_____
Class #4	_____	_____
Class #5	_____	_____
Class #6	_____	_____
Class #7	_____	_____

Meals   Water 8oz   Snacks   Water 8oz
1_____ ☐   1_____ ☐
2_____ ☐   2_____ ☐
3_____ ☐   Responsibilities, Chores, Homework ☐

SATURDAY ☺ 😲 😕 ☹ 😫 😐   **SUNDAY** ☺ 😲 😕 ☹ 😫 😐

Responsibility, Chores, Homework ☐   Responsibility, Chores, Homework ☐
_____   _____
_____   _____
_____   _____
_____   _____

GOALS

Weekly _____
_____

Monthly _____
_____

WEEK:_____/_____/20_____

MONDAY   I'm feeling: ☺ ☺ ☺ ☹ ☹ ☹

		Due Date
Class #1	_____	_____
Class #2	_____	_____
Class #3	_____	_____
Class #4	_____	_____
Class #5	_____	_____
Class #6	_____	_____
Class #7	_____	_____

Meals	Water 8oz	Snacks	Water 8oz
1_____	☐	1_____	☐
2_____	☐	2_____	☐
3_____	☐	Responsibilities, Chores, Homework	☐

TUESDAY   I'm feeling: ☺ ☺ ☺ ☹ ☹ ☹

		Due Date
Class #1	_____	_____
Class #2	_____	_____
Class #3	_____	_____
Class #4	_____	_____
Class #5	_____	_____
Class #6	_____	_____
Class #7	_____	_____

Meals	Water 8oz	Snacks	Water 8oz
1_____	☐	1_____	☐
2_____	☐	2_____	☐
3_____	☐	Responsibilities, Chores, Homework	☐

WEDNESDAY I'm feeling: ☺ ☺ ☺ ☹ ☹ ☹

		Due Date
Class #1	_____	_____
Class #2	_____	_____
Class #3	_____	_____
Class #4	_____	_____
Class #5	_____	_____
Class #6	_____	_____
Class #7	_____	_____

Meals	Water 8oz	Snacks	Water 8oz
1_____	☐	1_____	☐
2_____	☐	2_____	☐
3_____	☐	Responsibilities, Chores, Homework	☐

WEEK: _____ / _____ /20_____

THURSDAY I'm feeling: ☺ ☺ ☺ ☹ ☹ ☹

		Due Date
Class #1	_____	_____
Class #2	_____	_____
Class #3	_____	_____
Class #4	_____	_____
Class #5	_____	_____
Class #6	_____	_____
Class #7	_____	_____

Meals	Water 8oz	Snacks	Water 8oz
1_____	☐	1_____	☐
2_____	☐	2_____	☐
3_____	☐	Responsibilities, Chores, Homework	☐

FRIDAY I'm feeling: ☺ ☺ ☺ ☹ ☹ ☹

		Due Date
Class #1	_____	_____
Class #2	_____	_____
Class #3	_____	_____
Class #4	_____	_____
Class #5	_____	_____
Class #6	_____	_____
Class #7	_____	_____

Meals	Water 8oz	Snacks	Water 8oz
1_____	☐	1_____	☐
2_____	☐	2_____	☐
3_____	☐	Responsibilities, Chores, Homework	☐

SATURDAY ☺ ☺ ☺ ☹ ☹ ☹   SUNDAY ☺ ☺ ☺ ☹ ☹ ☹

Responsibility, Chores, Homework ☐	Responsibility, Chores, Homework ☐
_____	_____
_____	_____
_____	_____
_____	_____

GOALS

Weekly _____

Monthly _____

_____

WEEK: _____ / _____ /20 _____

MONDAY   I'm feeling: ☺ 😕 😐 ☹ 😣 😶

		Due Date
Class #1	_____	_____
Class #2	_____	_____
Class #3	_____	_____
Class #4	_____	_____
Class #5	_____	_____
Class #6	_____	_____
Class #7	_____	_____

Meals		Water 8oz	Snacks		Water 8oz
1	_____	☐	1	_____	☐
2	_____	☐	2	_____	☐
3	_____	☐	Responsibilities, Chores, Homework		☐

TUESDAY   I'm feeling: ☺ 😕 😐 ☹ 😣 😶

		Due Date
Class #1	_____	_____
Class #2	_____	_____
Class #3	_____	_____
Class #4	_____	_____
Class #5	_____	_____
Class #6	_____	_____
Class #7	_____	_____

Meals		Water 8oz	Snacks		Water 8oz
1	_____	☐	1	_____	☐
2	_____	☐	2	_____	☐
3	_____	☐	Responsibilities, Chores, Homework		☐

WEDNESDAY   I'm feeling: ☺ 😕 😐 ☹ 😣 😶

		Due Date
Class #1	_____	_____
Class #2	_____	_____
Class #3	_____	_____
Class #4	_____	_____
Class #5	_____	_____
Class #6	_____	_____
Class #7	_____	_____

Meals		Water 8oz	Snacks		Water 8oz
1	_____	☐	1	_____	☐
2	_____	☐	2	_____	☐
3	_____	☐	Responsibilities, Chores, Homework		☐

WEEK:_____/_____/20____

THURSDAY I'm feeling: ☺ 😐 😕 ☹ 😫 😑

Class #1 _____   Due Date
Class #2 _____   _____
Class #3 _____   _____
Class #4 _____   _____
Class #5 _____   _____
Class #6 _____   _____
Class #7 _____   _____

Meals   Water 8oz Snacks   Water 8oz
1_____   ☐ 1_____   ☐
2_____   ☐ 2_____   ☐
3_____   ☐ Responsibilities, Chores, Homework ☐

FRIDAY I'm feeling: ☺ 😐 😕 ☹ 😫 😑

Class #1 _____   Due Date
Class #2 _____   _____
Class #3 _____   _____
Class #4 _____   _____
Class #5 _____   _____
Class #6 _____   _____
Class #7 _____   _____

Meals   Water 8oz Snacks   Water 8oz
1_____   ☐ 1_____   ☐
2_____   ☐ 2_____   ☐
3_____   ☐ Responsibilities, Chores, Homework ☐

SATURDAY ☺ 😐 😕 ☹ 😫 😑   **SUNDAY** ☺ 😐 😕 ☹ 😫 😑

Responsibility, Chores, Homework ☐   Responsibility, Chores, Homework ☐

_____   _____
_____   _____
_____   _____
_____   _____

GOALS

Weekly _____
       _____

Monthly _____
        _____

WEEK: _____ / _____ /20_____

MONDAY I'm feeling: ☺ 😟 😵 😣 😬 😐

                                                                 Due Date

Class #1 _____ _____
Class #2 _____ _____
Class #3 _____ _____
Class #4 _____ _____
Class #5 _____ _____
Class #6 _____ _____
Class #7 _____ _____

Meals   Water 8oz Snacks   Water 8oz
1_____ ☐ 1_____ ☐
2_____ ☐ 2_____ ☐
3_____ ☐ Responsibilities, Chores, Homework ☐

TUESDAY I'm feeling: ☺ 😟 😵 😣 😬 😐

                                                                 Due Date

Class #1 _____ _____
Class #2 _____ _____
Class #3 _____ _____
Class #4 _____ _____
Class #5 _____ _____
Class #6 _____ _____
Class #7 _____ _____

Meals   Water 8oz Snacks   Water 8oz
1_____ ☐ 1_____ ☐
2_____ ☐ 2_____ ☐
3_____ ☐ Responsibilities, Chores, Homework ☐

WEDNESDAY I'm feeling: ☺ 😟 😵 😣 😬 😐

                                                                 Due Date

Class #1 _____ _____
Class #2 _____ _____
Class #3 _____ _____
Class #4 _____ _____
Class #5 _____ _____
Class #6 _____ _____
Class #7 _____ _____

Meals   Water 8oz Snacks   Water 8oz
1_____ ☐ 1_____ ☐
2_____ ☐ 2_____ ☐
3_____ ☐ Responsibilities, Chores, Homework ☐

WEEK:_____/_____/20_____

THURSDAY I'm feeling: 🙂 😐 😕 😟 😣 😶

		Due Date
Class #1	_____	_____
Class #2	_____	_____
Class #3	_____	_____
Class #4	_____	_____
Class #5	_____	_____
Class #6	_____	_____
Class #7	_____	_____

Meals   Water 8oz   Snacks   Water 8oz

1_____ ☐   1_____ ☐
2_____ ☐   2_____ ☐
3_____ ☐   Responsibilities, Chores, Homework ☐

FRIDAY I'm feeling: 🙂 😐 😕 😟 😣 😶

		Due Date
Class #1	_____	_____
Class #2	_____	_____
Class #3	_____	_____
Class #4	_____	_____
Class #5	_____	_____
Class #6	_____	_____
Class #7	_____	_____

Meals   Water 8oz   Snacks   Water 8oz

1_____ ☐   1_____ ☐
2_____ ☐   2_____ ☐
3_____ ☐   Responsibilities, Chores, Homework ☐

SATURDAY 🙂 😐 😕 😟 😣 😶   **SUNDAY** 🙂 😐 😕 😟 😣 😶

Responsibility, Chores, Homework ☐   Responsibility, Chores, Homework ☐

_____   _____
_____   _____
_____   _____
_____   _____

GOALS
Weekly _____
_____

Monthly _____
_____

WEEK: _____ / _____ /20_____

MONDAY   I'm feeling: ☺ 😶 😕 ☹ 😣 😐

		Due Date
Class #1	_____	_____
Class #2	_____	_____
Class #3	_____	_____
Class #4	_____	_____
Class #5	_____	_____
Class #6	_____	_____
Class #7	_____	_____

Meals   Water 8oz   Snacks   Water 8oz

1_____ ☐   1_____ ☐
2_____ ☐   2_____ ☐
3_____ ☐   Responsibilities, Chores, Homework ☐

TUESDAY   I'm feeling: ☺ 😶 😕 ☹ 😣 😐

		Due Date
Class #1	_____	_____
Class #2	_____	_____
Class #3	_____	_____
Class #4	_____	_____
Class #5	_____	_____
Class #6	_____	_____
Class #7	_____	_____

Meals   Water 8oz   Snacks   Water 8oz

1_____ ☐   1_____ ☐
2_____ ☐   2_____ ☐
3_____ ☐   Responsibilities, Chores, Homework ☐

WEDNESDAY I'm feeling: ☺ 😶 😕 ☹ 😣 😐

		Due Date
Class #1	_____	_____
Class #2	_____	_____
Class #3	_____	_____
Class #4	_____	_____
Class #5	_____	_____
Class #6	_____	_____
Class #7	_____	_____

Meals   Water 8oz   Snacks   Water 8oz

1_____ ☐   1_____ ☐
2_____ ☐   2_____ ☐
3_____ ☐   Responsibilities, Chores, Homework ☐

WEEK: _____ / _____ /20_____

THURSDAY I'm feeling: ☺ 😐 😕 ☹ 😣 😑

                                       Due Date

Class #1 _____ _____
Class #2 _____ _____
Class #3 _____ _____
Class #4 _____ _____
Class #5 _____ _____
Class #6 _____ _____
Class #7 _____ _____

Meals	Water 8oz	Snacks	Water 8oz
1_____	☐	1_____	☐
2_____	☐	2_____	☐
3_____	☐	Responsibilities, Chores, Homework	☐

FRIDAY I'm feeling: ☺ 😐 😕 ☹ 😣 😑

                                       Due Date

Class #1 _____ _____
Class #2 _____ _____
Class #3 _____ _____
Class #4 _____ _____
Class #5 _____ _____
Class #6 _____ _____
Class #7 _____ _____

Meals	Water 8oz	Snacks	Water 8oz
1_____	☐	1_____	☐
2_____	☐	2_____	☐
3_____	☐	Responsibilities, Chores, Homework	☐

SATURDAY ☺ 😐 😕 ☹ 😣 😑   **SUNDAY** ☺ 😐 😕 ☹ 😣 😑

Responsibility, Chores, Homework ☐   Responsibility, Chores, Homework ☐

_____ _____
_____ _____
_____ _____
_____ _____

GOALS

Weekly _____
_____

Monthly _____
_____

WEEK:_____/_____/20_____

MONDAY I'm feeling: ☺ ☺ ☹ ☹ ☹ ☹

		Due Date
Class #1	_____	_____
Class #2	_____	_____
Class #3	_____	_____
Class #4	_____	_____
Class #5	_____	_____
Class #6	_____	_____
Class #7	_____	_____

Meals	Water 8oz	Snacks	Water 8oz
1_____	☐	1_____	☐
2_____	☐	2_____	☐
3_____	☐	Responsibilities, Chores, Homework	☐

TUESDAY I'm feeling: ☺ ☺ ☹ ☹ ☹ ☹

		Due Date
Class #1	_____	_____
Class #2	_____	_____
Class #3	_____	_____
Class #4	_____	_____
Class #5	_____	_____
Class #6	_____	_____
Class #7	_____	_____

Meals	Water 8oz	Snacks	Water 8oz
1_____	☐	1_____	☐
2_____	☐	2_____	☐
3_____	☐	Responsibilities, Chores, Homework	☐

WEDNESDAY I'm feeling: ☺ ☺ ☹ ☹ ☹ ☹

		Due Date
Class #1	_____	_____
Class #2	_____	_____
Class #3	_____	_____
Class #4	_____	_____
Class #5	_____	_____
Class #6	_____	_____
Class #7	_____	_____

Meals	Water 8oz	Snacks	Water 8oz
1_____	☐	1_____	☐
2_____	☐	2_____	☐
3_____	☐	Responsibilities, Chores, Homework	☐

WEEK:_____/_____/20_____

THURSDAY I'm feeling: ☺ 😐 😕 ☹ 😣 😶

		Due Date
Class #1 _____		_____
Class #2 _____		_____
Class #3 _____		_____
Class #4 _____		_____
Class #5 _____		_____
Class #6 _____		_____
Class #7 _____		_____

Meals	Water 8oz	Snacks	Water 8oz
1_____	☐	1_____	☐
2_____	☐	2_____	☐
3_____	☐	Responsibilities, Chores, Homework	☐

FRIDAY I'm feeling: ☺ 😐 😕 ☹ 😣 😶

		Due Date
Class #1 _____		_____
Class #2 _____		_____
Class #3 _____		_____
Class #4 _____		_____
Class #5 _____		_____
Class #6 _____		_____
Class #7 _____		_____

Meals	Water 8oz	Snacks	Water 8oz
1_____	☐	1_____	☐
2_____	☐	2_____	☐
3_____	☐	Responsibilities, Chores, Homework	☐

SATURDAY ☺ 😐 😕 ☹ 😣 😶   **SUNDAY** ☺ 😐 😕 ☹ 😣 😶

Responsibility, Chores, Homework ☐	Responsibility, Chores, Homework ☐
_____	_____
_____	_____
_____	_____
_____	_____

GOALS

Weekly _____

_____

Monthly _____

_____

WEEK:_____/_____/20_____

MONDAY   I'm feeling: ☺ 😬 😕 ☹ 😣 😐

		Due Date
Class #1	_____	_____
Class #2	_____	_____
Class #3	_____	_____
Class #4	_____	_____
Class #5	_____	_____
Class #6	_____	_____
Class #7	_____	_____

Meals   Water 8oz   Snacks   Water 8oz
1_____ ☐   1_____ ☐
2_____ ☐   2_____ ☐
3_____ ☐   Responsibilities, Chores, Homework ☐

TUESDAY   I'm feeling: ☺ 😬 😕 ☹ 😣 😐

		Due Date
Class #1	_____	_____
Class #2	_____	_____
Class #3	_____	_____
Class #4	_____	_____
Class #5	_____	_____
Class #6	_____	_____
Class #7	_____	_____

Meals   Water 8oz   Snacks   Water 8oz
1_____ ☐   1_____ ☐
2_____ ☐   2_____ ☐
3_____ ☐   Responsibilities, Chores, Homework ☐

WEDNESDAY I'm feeling: ☺ 😬 😕 ☹ 😣 😐

		Due Date
Class #1	_____	_____
Class #2	_____	_____
Class #3	_____	_____
Class #4	_____	_____
Class #5	_____	_____
Class #6	_____	_____
Class #7	_____	_____

Meals   Water 8oz   Snacks   Water 8oz
1_____ ☐   1_____ ☐
2_____ ☐   2_____ ☐
3_____ ☐   Responsibilities, Chores, Homework ☐

WEEK:_____/_____/20_____

THURSDAY I'm feeling: ☺ 😐 😕 ☹ 😫 😣

Class #1 _____   Due Date
Class #2 _____   _____
Class #3 _____   _____
Class #4 _____   _____
Class #5 _____   _____
Class #6 _____   _____
Class #7 _____   _____

Meals   Water 8oz   Snacks   Water 8oz
1_____   ☐   1_____   ☐
2_____   ☐   2_____   ☐
3_____   ☐   Responsibilities, Chores, Homework ☐

FRIDAY I'm feeling: ☺ 😐 😕 ☹ 😫 😣

Class #1 _____   Due Date
Class #2 _____   _____
Class #3 _____   _____
Class #4 _____   _____
Class #5 _____   _____
Class #6 _____   _____
Class #7 _____   _____

Meals   Water 8oz   Snacks   Water 8oz
1_____   ☐   1_____   ☐
2_____   ☐   2_____   ☐
3_____   ☐   Responsibilities, Chores, Homework ☐

SATURDAY ☺ 😐 😕 ☹ 😫 😣   **SUNDAY** ☺ 😐 😕 ☹ 😫 😣

Responsibility, Chores, Homework ☐   Responsibility, Chores, Homework ☐
_____   _____
_____   _____
_____   _____
_____   _____

GOALS

Weekly _____

Monthly _____

WEEK:_____/_____/20_____

MONDAY I'm feeling: ☺ ☺ ☻ ☹ 😬 😐

		Due Date
Class #1	_____	_____
Class #2	_____	_____
Class #3	_____	_____
Class #4	_____	_____
Class #5	_____	_____
Class #6	_____	_____
Class #7	_____	_____

Meals	Water 8oz	Snacks	Water 8oz
1_____	☐	1_____	☐
2_____	☐	2_____	☐
3_____	☐	Responsibilities, Chores, Homework	☐

TUESDAY I'm feeling: ☺ ☺ ☻ ☹ 😬 😐

		Due Date
Class #1	_____	_____
Class #2	_____	_____
Class #3	_____	_____
Class #4	_____	_____
Class #5	_____	_____
Class #6	_____	_____
Class #7	_____	_____

Meals	Water 8oz	Snacks	Water 8oz
1_____	☐	1_____	☐
2_____	☐	2_____	☐
3_____	☐	Responsibilities, Chores, Homework	☐

WEDNESDAY I'm feeling: ☺ ☺ ☻ ☹ 😬 😐

		Due Date
Class #1	_____	_____
Class #2	_____	_____
Class #3	_____	_____
Class #4	_____	_____
Class #5	_____	_____
Class #6	_____	_____
Class #7	_____	_____

Meals	Water 8oz	Snacks	Water 8oz
1_____	☐	1_____	☐
2_____	☐	2_____	☐
3_____	☐	Responsibilities, Chores, Homework	☐

WEEK:_____/_____/20_____

THURSDAY I'm feeling: ☺ 😐 😕 ☹ 😤 😑

Due Date

Class #1 _____ _____
Class #2 _____ _____
Class #3 _____ _____
Class #4 _____ _____
Class #5 _____ _____
Class #6 _____ _____
Class #7 _____ _____

Meals	Water 8oz	Snacks	Water 8oz
1_____	☐	1_____	☐
2_____	☐	2_____	☐
3_____	☐	Responsibilities, Chores, Homework	☐

FRIDAY I'm feeling: ☺ 😐 😕 ☹ 😤 😑

Due Date

Class #1 _____ _____
Class #2 _____ _____
Class #3 _____ _____
Class #4 _____ _____
Class #5 _____ _____
Class #6 _____ _____
Class #7 _____ _____

Meals	Water 8oz	Snacks	Water 8oz
1_____	☐	1_____	☐
2_____	☐	2_____	☐
3_____	☐	Responsibilities, Chores, Homework	☐

SATURDAY ☺ 😐 😕 ☹ 😤 😑   SUNDAY ☺ 😐 😕 ☹ 😤 😑

Responsibility, Chores, Homework ☐   Responsibility, Chores, Homework ☐

_____   _____
_____   _____
_____   _____
_____   _____

GOALS
Weekly _____
_____
Monthly _____
_____

WEEK:_____/_____/20_____

MONDAY I'm feeling: ☺ 😕 😐 ☹ 😣 😔

	Due Date
Class #1 _____	_____
Class #2 _____	_____
Class #3 _____	_____
Class #4 _____	_____
Class #5 _____	_____
Class #6 _____	_____
Class #7 _____	_____

Meals   Water 8oz   Snacks   Water 8oz
1_____ ☐   1_____ ☐
2_____ ☐   2_____ ☐
3_____ ☐   Responsibilities, Chores, Homework ☐

TUESDAY I'm feeling: ☺ 😕 😐 ☹ 😣 😔

	Due Date
Class #1 _____	_____
Class #2 _____	_____
Class #3 _____	_____
Class #4 _____	_____
Class #5 _____	_____
Class #6 _____	_____
Class #7 _____	_____

Meals   Water 8oz   Snacks   Water 8oz
1_____ ☐   1_____ ☐
2_____ ☐   2_____ ☐
3_____ ☐   Responsibilities, Chores, Homework ☐

WEDNESDAY I'm feeling: ☺ 😕 😐 ☹ 😣 😔

	Due Date
Class #1 _____	_____
Class #2 _____	_____
Class #3 _____	_____
Class #4 _____	_____
Class #5 _____	_____
Class #6 _____	_____
Class #7 _____	_____

Meals   Water 8oz   Snacks   Water 8oz
1_____ ☐   1_____ ☐
2_____ ☐   2_____ ☐
3_____ ☐   Responsibilities, Chores, Homework ☐

WEEK: _____ / _____ /20_____

THURSDAY I'm feeling: ☺ 😐 😕 ☹ 😣 😑

		Due Date
Class #1	_____	_____
Class #2	_____	_____
Class #3	_____	_____
Class #4	_____	_____
Class #5	_____	_____
Class #6	_____	_____
Class #7	_____	_____

Meals	Water 8oz	Snacks	Water 8oz
1_____	☐	1_____	☐
2_____	☐	2_____	☐
3_____	☐	Responsibilities, Chores, Homework	☐

FRIDAY I'm feeling: ☺ 😐 😕 ☹ 😣 😑

		Due Date
Class #1	_____	_____
Class #2	_____	_____
Class #3	_____	_____
Class #4	_____	_____
Class #5	_____	_____
Class #6	_____	_____
Class #7	_____	_____

Meals	Water 8oz	Snacks	Water 8oz
1_____	☐	1_____	☐
2_____	☐	2_____	☐
3_____	☐	Responsibilities, Chores, Homework	☐

SATURDAY ☺ 😐 😕 ☹ 😣 😑   SUNDAY ☺ 😐 😕 ☹ 😣 😑

Responsibility, Chores, Homework ☐	Responsibility, Chores, Homework ☐
_____	_____
_____	_____
_____	_____
_____	_____

GOALS

Weekly _____

Monthly _____

WEEK:_____/_____/20_____

MONDAY I'm feeling: 🙂 😯 😐 🙁 😬 😕

		Due Date
Class #1	_____	_____
Class #2	_____	_____
Class #3	_____	_____
Class #4	_____	_____
Class #5	_____	_____
Class #6	_____	_____
Class #7	_____	_____

Meals	Water 8oz	Snacks	Water 8oz
1_____	☐	1_____	☐
2_____	☐	2_____	☐
3_____	☐	Responsibilities, Chores, Homework	☐

TUESDAY I'm feeling: 🙂 😯 😐 🙁 😬 😕

		Due Date
Class #1	_____	_____
Class #2	_____	_____
Class #3	_____	_____
Class #4	_____	_____
Class #5	_____	_____
Class #6	_____	_____
Class #7	_____	_____

Meals	Water 8oz	Snacks	Water 8oz
1_____	☐	1_____	☐
2_____	☐	2_____	☐
3_____	☐	Responsibilities, Chores, Homework	☐

WEDNESDAY I'm feeling: 🙂 😯 😐 🙁 😬 😕

		Due Date
Class #1	_____	_____
Class #2	_____	_____
Class #3	_____	_____
Class #4	_____	_____
Class #5	_____	_____
Class #6	_____	_____
Class #7	_____	_____

Meals	Water 8oz	Snacks	Water 8oz
1_____	☐	1_____	☐
2_____	☐	2_____	☐
3_____	☐	Responsibilities, Chores, Homework	☐

WEEK:____/_____/20____

THURSDAY I'm feeling: ☺ 😐 😕 ☹ 😫 😖

		Due Date
Class #1 _____		_____
Class #2 _____		_____
Class #3 _____		_____
Class #4 _____		_____
Class #5 _____		_____
Class #6 _____		_____
Class #7 _____		_____

Meals	Water 8oz	Snacks	Water 8oz
1_____	☐	1_____	☐
2_____	☐	2_____	☐
3_____	☐	Responsibilities, Chores, Homework	☐

FRIDAY I'm feeling: ☺ 😐 😕 ☹ 😫 😖

		Due Date
Class #1 _____		_____
Class #2 _____		_____
Class #3 _____		_____
Class #4 _____		_____
Class #5 _____		_____
Class #6 _____		_____
Class #7 _____		_____

Meals	Water 8oz	Snacks	Water 8oz
1_____	☐	1_____	☐
2_____	☐	2_____	☐
3_____	☐	Responsibilities, Chores, Homework	☐

SATURDAY ☺ 😐 😕 ☹ 😫 😖   **SUNDAY** ☺ 😐 😕 ☹ 😫 😖

Responsibility, Chores, Homework ☐	Responsibility, Chores, Homework ☐
_____	_____
_____	_____
_____	_____
_____	_____

GOALS

Weekly _____

_____

Monthly _____

_____

WEEK: _____ / _____ / 20 _____

MONDAY   I'm feeling: ☺ 😐 😣 🙁 😬 😕

		Due Date
Class #1	_____	_____
Class #2	_____	_____
Class #3	_____	_____
Class #4	_____	_____
Class #5	_____	_____
Class #6	_____	_____
Class #7	_____	_____

Meals	Water 8oz	Snacks	Water 8oz
1_____	☐	1_____	☐
2_____	☐	2_____	☐
3_____	☐	Responsibilities, Chores, Homework	☐

TUESDAY   I'm feeling: ☺ 😐 😣 🙁 😬 😕

		Due Date
Class #1	_____	_____
Class #2	_____	_____
Class #3	_____	_____
Class #4	_____	_____
Class #5	_____	_____
Class #6	_____	_____
Class #7	_____	_____

Meals	Water 8oz	Snacks	Water 8oz
1_____	☐	1_____	☐
2_____	☐	2_____	☐
3_____	☐	Responsibilities, Chores, Homework	☐

WEDNESDAY   I'm feeling: ☺ 😐 😣 🙁 😬 😕

		Due Date
Class #1	_____	_____
Class #2	_____	_____
Class #3	_____	_____
Class #4	_____	_____
Class #5	_____	_____
Class #6	_____	_____
Class #7	_____	_____

Meals	Water 8oz	Snacks	Water 8oz
1_____	☐	1_____	☐
2_____	☐	2_____	☐
3_____	☐	Responsibilities, Chores, Homework	☐

WEEK: _____ / _____ /20_____

THURSDAY   I'm feeling: 😊 😐 🙁 😟 😣 😶

		Due Date
Class #1	_____	_____
Class #2	_____	_____
Class #3	_____	_____
Class #4	_____	_____
Class #5	_____	_____
Class #6	_____	_____
Class #7	_____	_____

Meals	Water 8oz	Snacks	Water 8oz
1_____	☐	1_____	☐
2_____	☐	2_____	☐
3_____	☐	Responsibilities, Chores, Homework	☐

FRIDAY   I'm feeling: 😊 😐 🙁 😟 😣 😶

		Due Date
Class #1	_____	_____
Class #2	_____	_____
Class #3	_____	_____
Class #4	_____	_____
Class #5	_____	_____
Class #6	_____	_____
Class #7	_____	_____

Meals	Water 8oz	Snacks	Water 8oz
1_____	☐	1_____	☐
2_____	☐	2_____	☐
3_____	☐	Responsibilities, Chores, Homework	☐

SATURDAY 😊 😐 🙁 😟 😣 😶   SUNDAY 😊 😐 🙁 😟 😣 😶

Responsibility, Chores, Homework ☐	Responsibility, Chores, Homework ☐
_____	_____
_____	_____
_____	_____
_____	_____

GOALS
Weekly   _____

Monthly _____

WEEK: _____ / _____ /20 _____

MONDAY I'm feeling: ☺ 😮 😕 ☹ 😣 😐

Class #1 _____ Due Date
Class #2 _____ _____
Class #3 _____ _____
Class #4 _____ _____
Class #5 _____ _____
Class #6 _____ _____
Class #7 _____

Meals   Water 8oz   Snacks   Water 8oz
1_____ ☐ 1_____ ☐
2_____ ☐ 2_____ ☐
3_____ ☐ Responsibilities, Chores, Homework ☐

TUESDAY I'm feeling: ☺ 😮 😕 ☹ 😣 😐

Class #1 _____ Due Date
Class #2 _____ _____
Class #3 _____ _____
Class #4 _____ _____
Class #5 _____ _____
Class #6 _____ _____
Class #7 _____

Meals   Water 8oz   Snacks   Water 8oz
1_____ ☐ 1_____ ☐
2_____ ☐ 2_____ ☐
3_____ ☐ Responsibilities, Chores, Homework ☐

WEDNESDAY I'm feeling: ☺ 😮 😕 ☹ 😣 😐

Class #1 _____ Due Date
Class #2 _____ _____
Class #3 _____ _____
Class #4 _____ _____
Class #5 _____ _____
Class #6 _____ _____
Class #7 _____

Meals   Water 8oz   Snacks   Water 8oz
1_____ ☐ 1_____ ☐
2_____ ☐ 2_____ ☐
3_____ ☐ Responsibilities, Chores, Homework ☐

WEEK:_____/_____/20_____

THURSDAY I'm feeling: ☺ 😐 😕 ☹ 😫 😑

		Due Date
Class #1 _____		_____
Class #2 _____		_____
Class #3 _____		_____
Class #4 _____		_____
Class #5 _____		_____
Class #6 _____		_____
Class #7 _____		_____

Meals	Water 8oz	Snacks	Water 8oz
1_____	☐	1_____	☐
2_____	☐	2_____	☐
3_____	☐	Responsibilities, Chores, Homework	☐

FRIDAY I'm feeling: ☺ 😐 😕 ☹ 😫 😑

		Due Date
Class #1 _____		_____
Class #2 _____		_____
Class #3 _____		_____
Class #4 _____		_____
Class #5 _____		_____
Class #6 _____		_____
Class #7 _____		_____

Meals	Water 8oz	Snacks	Water 8oz
1_____	☐	1_____	☐
2_____	☐	2_____	☐
3_____	☐	Responsibilities, Chores, Homework	☐

SATURDAY ☺ 😐 😕 ☹ 😫 😑   **SUNDAY** ☺ 😐 😕 ☹ 😫 😑

Responsibility, Chores, Homework ☐	Responsibility, Chores, Homework ☐
_____	_____
_____	_____
_____	_____
_____	_____

GOALS

Weekly _____

Monthly _____

WEEK:_____/_____/20_____

MONDAY I'm feeling: ☺ 😯 😕 ☹ 😣 😐

		Due Date
Class #1	_____	_____
Class #2	_____	_____
Class #3	_____	_____
Class #4	_____	_____
Class #5	_____	_____
Class #6	_____	_____
Class #7	_____	_____

Meals	Water 8oz	Snacks	Water 8oz
1_____	☐	1_____	☐
2_____	☐	2_____	☐
3_____	☐	Responsibilities, Chores, Homework	☐

TUESDAY I'm feeling: ☺ 😯 😕 ☹ 😣 😐

		Due Date
Class #1	_____	_____
Class #2	_____	_____
Class #3	_____	_____
Class #4	_____	_____
Class #5	_____	_____
Class #6	_____	_____
Class #7	_____	_____

Meals	Water 8oz	Snacks	Water 8oz
1_____	☐	1_____	☐
2_____	☐	2_____	☐
3_____	☐	Responsibilities, Chores, Homework	☐

WEDNESDAY I'm feeling: ☺ 😯 😕 ☹ 😣 😐

		Due Date
Class #1	_____	_____
Class #2	_____	_____
Class #3	_____	_____
Class #4	_____	_____
Class #5	_____	_____
Class #6	_____	_____
Class #7	_____	_____

Meals	Water 8oz	Snacks	Water 8oz
1_____	☐	1_____	☐
2_____	☐	2_____	☐
3_____	☐	Responsibilities, Chores, Homework	☐

WEEK:_____/_____/20_____

THURSDAY I'm feeling: ☺ ☺ ☺ ☹ 😤 😐

		Due Date
Class #1 _____		_____
Class #2 _____		_____
Class #3 _____		_____
Class #4 _____		_____
Class #5 _____		_____
Class #6 _____		_____
Class #7 _____		_____

Meals	Water 8oz	Snacks	Water 8oz
1_____	☐	1_____	☐
2_____	☐	2_____	☐
3_____	☐	Responsibilities, Chores, Homework	☐

FRIDAY I'm feeling: ☺ ☺ ☺ ☹ 😤 😐

		Due Date
Class #1 _____		_____
Class #2 _____		_____
Class #3 _____		_____
Class #4 _____		_____
Class #5 _____		_____
Class #6 _____		_____
Class #7 _____		_____

Meals	Water 8oz	Snacks	Water 8oz
1_____	☐	1_____	☐
2_____	☐	2_____	☐
3_____	☐	Responsibilities, Chores, Homework	☐

SATURDAY ☺ ☺ ☺ ☹ 😤 😐   SUNDAY ☺ ☺ ☺ ☹ 😤 😐

Responsibility, Chores, Homework ☐	Responsibility, Chores, Homework ☐
_____	_____
_____	_____
_____	_____
_____	_____

GOALS
Weekly _____

Monthly _____

WEEK: _____ / _____ /20_____

MONDAY I'm feeling: ☺ 😐 😕 ☹ 😣 😑

		Due Date
Class #1	_____	_____
Class #2	_____	_____
Class #3	_____	_____
Class #4	_____	_____
Class #5	_____	_____
Class #6	_____	_____
Class #7	_____	_____

Meals   Water 8oz   Snacks   Water 8oz
1_____   ☐   1_____   ☐
2_____   ☐   2_____   ☐
3_____   ☐   Responsibilities, Chores, Homework   ☐

TUESDAY I'm feeling: ☺ 😐 😕 ☹ 😣 😑

		Due Date
Class #1	_____	_____
Class #2	_____	_____
Class #3	_____	_____
Class #4	_____	_____
Class #5	_____	_____
Class #6	_____	_____
Class #7	_____	_____

Meals   Water 8oz   Snacks   Water 8oz
1_____   ☐   1_____   ☐
2_____   ☐   2_____   ☐
3_____   ☐   Responsibilities, Chores, Homework   ☐

WEDNESDAY I'm feeling: ☺ 😐 😕 ☹ 😣 😑

		Due Date
Class #1	_____	_____
Class #2	_____	_____
Class #3	_____	_____
Class #4	_____	_____
Class #5	_____	_____
Class #6	_____	_____
Class #7	_____	_____

Meals   Water 8oz   Snacks   Water 8oz
1_____   ☐   1_____   ☐
2_____   ☐   2_____   ☐
3_____   ☐   Responsibilities, Chores, Homework   ☐

WEEK: _____ / _____ /20_____

THURSDAY I'm feeling: 🙂 😯 😐 ☹️ 😣 😑

Due Date

Class #1 _____ _____
Class #2 _____ _____
Class #3 _____ _____
Class #4 _____ _____
Class #5 _____ _____
Class #6 _____ _____
Class #7 _____

Meals   Water 8oz   Snacks   Water 8oz
1_____ ☐   1_____ ☐
2_____ ☐   2_____ ☐
3_____ ☐   Responsibilities, Chores, Homework ☐

FRIDAY I'm feeling: 🙂 😯 😐 ☹️ 😣 😑

Due Date

Class #1 _____ _____
Class #2 _____ _____
Class #3 _____ _____
Class #4 _____ _____
Class #5 _____ _____
Class #6 _____ _____
Class #7 _____

Meals   Water 8oz   Snacks   Water 8oz
1_____ ☐   1_____ ☐
2_____ ☐   2_____ ☐
3_____ ☐   Responsibilities, Chores, Homework ☐

SATURDAY 🙂 😯 😐 ☹️ 😣 😑   **SUNDAY** 🙂 😯 😐 ☹️ 😣 😑

Responsibility, Chores, Homework ☐   Responsibility, Chores, Homework ☐

_____   _____
_____   _____
_____   _____
_____   _____

GOALS
Weekly _____
        _____
Monthly _____
        _____

WEEK: _____ / _____ /20____

MONDAY   I'm feeling: ☺ 😐 😟 ☹ 😣 😑

                                                 Due Date

Class #1 _____   _____
Class #2 _____   _____
Class #3 _____   _____
Class #4 _____   _____
Class #5 _____   _____
Class #6 _____   _____
Class #7 _____   _____

Meals   Water 8oz   Snacks   Water 8oz
1_____ ☐   1_____ ☐
2_____ ☐   2_____ ☐
3_____ ☐   Responsibilities, Chores, Homework ☐

TUESDAY   I'm feeling: ☺ 😐 😟 ☹ 😣 😑

                                                 Due Date

Class #1 _____   _____
Class #2 _____   _____
Class #3 _____   _____
Class #4 _____   _____
Class #5 _____   _____
Class #6 _____   _____
Class #7 _____   _____

Meals   Water 8oz   Snacks   Water 8oz
1_____ ☐   1_____ ☐
2_____ ☐   2_____ ☐
3_____ ☐   Responsibilities, Chores, Homework ☐

WEDNESDAY I'm feeling: ☺ 😐 😟 ☹ 😣 😑

                                                 Due Date

Class #1 _____   _____
Class #2 _____   _____
Class #3 _____   _____
Class #4 _____   _____
Class #5 _____   _____
Class #6 _____   _____
Class #7 _____   _____

Meals   Water 8oz   Snacks   Water 8oz
1_____ ☐   1_____ ☐
2_____ ☐   2_____ ☐
3_____ ☐   Responsibilities, Chores, Homework ☐

WEEK:_____/_____/20_____

THURSDAY   I'm feeling: ☺ 😐 😕 😠 😫 😑

		Due Date
Class #1	_____	_____
Class #2	_____	_____
Class #3	_____	_____
Class #4	_____	_____
Class #5	_____	_____
Class #6	_____	_____
Class #7	_____	_____

Meals	Water 8oz	Snacks	Water 8oz
1_____	☐	1_____	☐
2_____	☐	2_____	☐
3_____	☐	Responsibilities, Chores, Homework	☐

FRIDAY   I'm feeling: ☺ 😐 😕 😠 😫 😑

		Due Date
Class #1	_____	_____
Class #2	_____	_____
Class #3	_____	_____
Class #4	_____	_____
Class #5	_____	_____
Class #6	_____	_____
Class #7	_____	_____

Meals	Water 8oz	Snacks	Water 8oz
1_____	☐	1_____	☐
2_____	☐	2_____	☐
3_____	☐	Responsibilities, Chores, Homework	☐

SATURDAY ☺ 😐 😕 😠 😫 😑   **SUNDAY** ☺ 😐 😕 😠 😫 😑

Responsibility, Chores, Homework ☐   Responsibility, Chores, Homework ☐

_____   _____
_____   _____
_____   _____
_____   _____

GOALS

Weekly _____

_____

Monthly _____

_____

WEEK:_____/_____/20_____

MONDAY I'm feeling: ☺ 😕 😣 😖 😫 😐

		Due Date
Class #1	_____	_____
Class #2	_____	_____
Class #3	_____	_____
Class #4	_____	_____
Class #5	_____	_____
Class #6	_____	_____
Class #7	_____	_____

Meals   Water 8oz   Snacks   Water 8oz
1_____ ☐   1_____ ☐
2_____ ☐   2_____ ☐
3_____ ☐   Responsibilities, Chores, Homework ☐

TUESDAY I'm feeling: ☺ 😕 😣 😖 😫 😐

		Due Date
Class #1	_____	_____
Class #2	_____	_____
Class #3	_____	_____
Class #4	_____	_____
Class #5	_____	_____
Class #6	_____	_____
Class #7	_____	_____

Meals   Water 8oz   Snacks   Water 8oz
1_____ ☐   1_____ ☐
2_____ ☐   2_____ ☐
3_____ ☐   Responsibilities, Chores, Homework ☐

WEDNESDAY I'm feeling: ☺ 😕 😣 😖 😫 😐

		Due Date
Class #1	_____	_____
Class #2	_____	_____
Class #3	_____	_____
Class #4	_____	_____
Class #5	_____	_____
Class #6	_____	_____
Class #7	_____	_____

Meals   Water 8oz   Snacks   Water 8oz
1_____ ☐   1_____ ☐
2_____ ☐   2_____ ☐
3_____ ☐   Responsibilities, Chores, Homework ☐

WEEK:_____/_____/20_____

THURSDAY I'm feeling: ☺ 😕 😐 ☹ 😫 😐

Due Date

Class #1 _____ _____
Class #2 _____ _____
Class #3 _____ _____
Class #4 _____ _____
Class #5 _____ _____
Class #6 _____ _____
Class #7 _____ _____

Meals   Water 8oz Snacks   Water 8oz
1_____ ☐ 1_____ ☐
2_____ ☐ 2_____ ☐
3_____ ☐ Responsibilities, Chores, Homework ☐

FRIDAY I'm feeling: ☺ 😕 😐 ☹ 😫 😐

Due Date

Class #1 _____ _____
Class #2 _____ _____
Class #3 _____ _____
Class #4 _____ _____
Class #5 _____ _____
Class #6 _____ _____
Class #7 _____ _____

Meals   Water 8oz Snacks   Water 8oz
1_____ ☐ 1_____ ☐
2_____ ☐ 2_____ ☐
3_____ ☐ Responsibilities, Chores, Homework ☐

SATURDAY ☺ 😕 😐 ☹ 😫 😐   **SUNDAY** ☺ 😕 😐 ☹ 😫 😐

Responsibility, Chores, Homework ____ ☐   Responsibility, Chores, Homework ____ ☐
_____   _____
_____   _____
_____   _____
_____   _____

GOALS

Weekly _____

Monthly _____
_____

WEEK:_____/_____/20_____

MONDAY I'm feeling: 🙂 😐 😣 😟 😫 😶

Due Date

Class #1 _____ _____
Class #2 _____ _____
Class #3 _____ _____
Class #4 _____ _____
Class #5 _____ _____
Class #6 _____ _____
Class #7 _____ _____

Meals   Water 8oz   Snacks   Water 8oz
1_____   ☐   1_____   ☐
2_____   ☐   2_____   ☐
3_____   ☐   Responsibilities, Chores, Homework   ☐

TUESDAY I'm feeling: 🙂 😐 😣 😟 😫 😶

Due Date

Class #1 _____ _____
Class #2 _____ _____
Class #3 _____ _____
Class #4 _____ _____
Class #5 _____ _____
Class #6 _____ _____
Class #7 _____ _____

Meals   Water 8oz   Snacks   Water 8oz
1_____   ☐   1_____   ☐
2_____   ☐   2_____   ☐
3_____   ☐   Responsibilities, Chores, Homework   ☐

WEDNESDAY I'm feeling: 🙂 😐 😣 😟 😫 😶

Due Date

Class #1 _____ _____
Class #2 _____ _____
Class #3 _____ _____
Class #4 _____ _____
Class #5 _____ _____
Class #6 _____ _____
Class #7 _____ _____

Meals   Water 8oz   Snacks   Water 8oz
1_____   ☐   1_____   ☐
2_____   ☐   2_____   ☐
3_____   ☐   Responsibilities, Chores, Homework   ☐

WEEK:_____ / _____/20_____

THURSDAY I'm feeling: ☺ 😬 😕 ☹ 😣 😐

		Due Date
Class #1 _____		_____
Class #2 _____		_____
Class #3 _____		_____
Class #4 _____		_____
Class #5 _____		_____
Class #6 _____		_____
Class #7 _____		_____

Meals	Water 8oz	Snacks	Water 8oz
1_____	☐	1_____	☐
2_____	☐	2_____	☐
3_____	☐	Responsibilities, Chores, Homework	☐

FRIDAY I'm feeling: ☺ 😬 😕 ☹ 😣 😐

		Due Date
Class #1 _____		_____
Class #2 _____		_____
Class #3 _____		_____
Class #4 _____		_____
Class #5 _____		_____
Class #6 _____		_____
Class #7 _____		_____

Meals	Water 8oz	Snacks	Water 8oz
1_____	☐	1_____	☐
2_____	☐	2_____	☐
3_____	☐	Responsibilities, Chores, Homework	☐

SATURDAY ☺ 😬 😕 ☹ 😣 😐   ## SUNDAY ☺ 😬 😕 ☹ 😣 😐

Responsibility, Chores, Homework ☐	Responsibility, Chores, Homework ☐
_____	_____
_____	_____
_____	_____
_____	_____

GOALS
Weekly _____

Monthly _____

WEEK:_____/_____/20_____

MONDAY I'm feeling: ☺ 😐 😕 ☹ 😫 😶

		Due Date
Class #1 _____		_____
Class #2 _____		_____
Class #3 _____		_____
Class #4 _____		_____
Class #5 _____		_____
Class #6 _____		_____
Class #7 _____		_____

Meals	Water 8oz	Snacks	Water 8oz
1_____	☐	1_____	☐
2_____	☐	2_____	☐
3_____	☐	Responsibilities, Chores, Homework	☐

TUESDAY I'm feeling: ☺ 😐 😕 ☹ 😫 😶

		Due Date
Class #1 _____		_____
Class #2 _____		_____
Class #3 _____		_____
Class #4 _____		_____
Class #5 _____		_____
Class #6 _____		_____
Class #7 _____		_____

Meals	Water 8oz	Snacks	Water 8oz
1_____	☐	1_____	☐
2_____	☐	2_____	☐
3_____	☐	Responsibilities, Chores, Homework	☐

WEDNESDAY I'm feeling: ☺ 😐 😕 ☹ 😫 😶

		Due Date
Class #1 _____		_____
Class #2 _____		_____
Class #3 _____		_____
Class #4 _____		_____
Class #5 _____		_____
Class #6 _____		_____
Class #7 _____		_____

Meals	Water 8oz	Snacks	Water 8oz
1_____	☐	1_____	☐
2_____	☐	2_____	☐
3_____	☐	Responsibilities, Chores, Homework	☐

WEEK: _____ / _____ /20_____

THURSDAY I'm feeling: ☺ 😕 😐 ☹ 😣 😑

		Due Date
Class #1	_____	_____
Class #2	_____	_____
Class #3	_____	_____
Class #4	_____	_____
Class #5	_____	_____
Class #6	_____	_____
Class #7	_____	_____

Meals   Water 8oz   Snacks   Water 8oz
1_____ ☐ 1_____ ☐
2_____ ☐ 2_____ ☐
3_____ ☐ Responsibilities, Chores, Homework ☐

FRIDAY I'm feeling: ☺ 😕 😐 ☹ 😣 😑

		Due Date
Class #1	_____	_____
Class #2	_____	_____
Class #3	_____	_____
Class #4	_____	_____
Class #5	_____	_____
Class #6	_____	_____
Class #7	_____	_____

Meals   Water 8oz   Snacks   Water 8oz
1_____ ☐ 1_____ ☐
2_____ ☐ 2_____ ☐
3_____ ☐ Responsibilities, Chores, Homework ☐

SATURDAY ☺ 😕 😐 ☹ 😣 😑   SUNDAY ☺ 😕 😐 ☹ 😣 😑

Responsibility, Chores, Homework ☐   Responsibility, Chores, Homework ☐

_____   _____
_____   _____
_____   _____
_____   _____

GOALS
Weekly _____
        _____
Monthly _____
        _____

SOURCES

Chapter 9: Restorative Practices
"International Institute for Restorative Practices." Welcome to International Institute for Restorative Practices. Web. 14 Sept. 2011. <http://www.iirp.edu/whatisrp.php>.

Chapter 12: Daniel Puder's Outlook on Bullying
"Students Against Violence Everywhere-Dealing with Bullies without Making Things Worse." SAVE (Students Against Violence everywhere), Violence Prevention Program, School Violence. Web. 19 Sept. 2011. <http://www.nationalsave.org/main/bully.php>.

"What Parents and Kids Need to Know about Bullying-Hazelden." Hazelden Addiction Treatment Center. Web. 04 Sept. 2011. <http://www.hazelden.org/web/public/prev40109.page>.

Chapter 15: Lifestyle
Susan Villani, M.D. *"Impact of Media on Children and Adolescents: A 10-Year Review of the Research"*